IV26

CU00798515

"THE CAIRN LINE OF STEAMSHIPS COMPANY LIMITED"

1876 - 2005

GILBERT T. WALLACE

Derek Porter

Warmest regards.

Gil Wallace

29.07.05

"THE CAIRN LINE OF STEAMSHIPS COMPANY LIMITED"
1876 - 2005

GILBERT T. WALLACE

Cairn Line Cap Badge

Copyright:

First Published 2005

ISBN 0-9550078-0-1

© Gilbert T. Wallace 2005

All rights reserved.

No part of this publication may be reproduced or stored in any form
without the prior permission of the copyright holder.

Published by:

Gilbert T. Wallace
3 Milton Gardens South
Edinburgh
Midlothian
Scotland
EH15 3PG

Formatted, printed and bound by:
Lothian Print Ltd.
7 New Lairdship Yards
Broomhouse Road
Edinburgh
EH11 3UY

CONTENTS

DEDICATION

DEDICATED TO MY SISTER,
SYBIL VEITCH WALLACE,
WHO HAS A SMILE FOR EVERYONE
AND MY GRANDCHILDREN
WILLIAM ROBERT WALLACE
AND
DAISY CATHERINE WALLACE

AFORETHOUGHT

"I CONTINUE TO BE AMAZED AND HUMBLED BY THE
GREAT GALLANTRY AND GOOD HUMOUR OF MERCHANT NAVY
PERSONNEL DURING THE YEARS OF WAR."

Captain William W.F. Chattern Dickson,
Royal Navy, Retired
24th June 2001

Captain Dickson is the author of the 'Seedie's List of Awards to the Merchant Navy'. He served in the RN between 1945 and 1986. His service was mainly in the UK and Far East. His last two appointments as a Captain were, Naval Attache in New Delhi from 1980 to 1982, and then in command of HMS MERCURY, which was the RN Signal School.

AUTHOR

Gilbert T. Wallace was born on 20th February 1934 in Newhaven, Edinburgh and was one of five children. Their father was a police officer and in 1937 the family moved from Leith to Portobello, Edinburgh.

The author attended Portobello Primary and Secondary Higher School. Where he took up Navigation and Seamanship subjects; one of the few state schools in the United Kingdom that taught nautical subjects. Leaving school in 1949.

Whilst waiting to enrol into Leith Nautical College, he obtained a job as a petrol pump attendant at Bell Watt's Garage in Duke Street, Leith and also attended Leith Academy School (night school) for technical subjects including drawing.

Author – 16 year old cadet – CAIRNESK (III)

Later in 1949, he attended TS Dolphin Leith Docks and Leith Nautical College, Commercial Street, Leith for a years course and later joined The Cairn Line of Steamships Company Limited, Milburn House, Newcastle-upon-Tyne as a cadet in 1950 until 1954. He later served in the Royal Air Force (Provost) Police, the Edinburgh City Police later to be known as Lothians & Borders Police and the Crown Office, Edinburgh.

The Author finally retired in 1998 when he took up the hobby of oil and watercolour painting.

TS DOLPHIN – Leith Docks – Circa 1950's

ACKNOWLEDGEMENTS

I would like to acknowledge with special thanks all persons who assisted me with their excellent knowledge and valuable time in collating and compiling facts towards perfecting the history of the Cairn Line of Steamships.

In particular, Michael Baxter, who came to my aid on many occasions with his invaluable knowledge of the Mercantile Marine and the research carried out by him on my behalf.

Other personnel are Eric Eagle, David Atkinson, Alan Fairley, David Burrell, Richard Alexander, Paul Edwards, Michael Jack, Gayle Robinson, Michael Jordan, John Landels, Alexander Harvey, Alastair Anderson, Peter Wallace, L.A. Smith, J.L. Loughran, Roy Fenton, Dorothy Cunningham, Hubert Hall, George Robinson, and Marion Foster.

The following names are personnel from whom I gained information and allowed me to research their books etc, possibly to a lesser degree, but just as informative and valuable, thus enhancing the company's history. In some instances I could not trace the authors, but I have acknowledged their source.

Staff of the following libraries, museums etc

Aberdeen City Council

Archives of Newfoundland & Labrador, St John's, Newfoundland

Central Library, Dundee

George IV Bridge, Edinburgh

Glasgow University Archives

Libraries & Guildhall Art Gallery, London

Maritime Museum of the Atlantic, Halifax, Nova Scotia

Maritime Museum, Greenwich, London

Memorial University of Newfoundland

Newcastle-upon-Tyne

Piershill, Edinburgh

Scottish National Library, Edinburgh

The Mitchell Library, Glasgow City Council

Trinity House, Leith

Tyne & Wear Library, Newcastle-upon-Tyne

Vancouver Maritime Museum

Also:

Ian McMurtrie, Andrew C Douglas, Neil Hindmarsh, Ilene McIvor, Norman Middlemas, Margaret P Marr, J Henderson, Duncan Haws, Joseph Bell, John Band, Charles Sutherland, Alan & Nancy Stobbs, J Clarkson, AJ Blackler, CL Reynolds and Peter Myers.

And Including:

A J Tennant (Author of "British Merchant Ships Sunk by the German U-Boats")

Captain W W F Chattern Dickson (Author of "Seedie's List of Awards to the Merchant Navy")

D C Thomson & Co Ltd, Dundee. (Mr C G Laird & Mr Douglas Murray)

Fotoflite, Ashford, Kent

Furness Withy & Co Ltd

Furness Withy Group

Graeme Somner (Author of "70 North to 70 South – A History of the Christian Salvesen Fleet)

Paul Lund & Harry Ludlum (Authors of "Night of the U-Boats, Convoy SC7")

Peter Collins (Author of "The Illustrated Dictionary of North East Shipwrecks")

Philip N Thomas (Author of "British Steam Tramps – Vols. 1 & 2)

Rear Admiral John Lang (Report in Times Newspaper – Accidents)

Scotsman Publications (Mr Brady)

Sydney C Heal (Author of "The Canadian Forts & Parks")

Tradewind Models (A Fancy)

Vice Admiral G Campbell & Mr IO Evans (Authors of "Book of Flags")

Credits for the photographs are given along with the appropriate entitlement, where the owner of the copyright is known. When not known, attempts were made to trace and obtain permission to re-produce and to give due credit. It is inevitable, particularly with older photographs, that a few credits are omitted, but unintentionally. If this is the case, I offer my sincere apologies.

FRONT COVER DESIGN; MILBURN HOUSE

PHOTOGRAPH; FUNNELS, FLAGS, BY AUTHOR.

BACK COVER; CAIRNESK (III) PAINTING – NORTH WESTERLY, BY P WHITTOCK ARTIST, PERMISSION OF ALAN FAIRLEY.

APPENDIX 1 & 2 BY PETER WALLACE *(NO RELATION)*.

APPENDIX 3 BY MIKE BAXTER

INTRODUCTION

In 2000, I thought of researching the history of the Cairn Line of Steamships Co Ltd, Milburn House, Newcastle upon Tyne because of my past association. I have, in time, wondered how the Company fared in the 'reducing movement' of the British Mercantile Marine. In 1876, Starks and Cairns were formed as Ship Brokers. Later, from 1883 to 1908, the Cairn Line had built or purchased 22 ships. There were 21 'Cairn' ships and one other named KEROULA.

Cairn Steamships Line acquired the Thomson Line of Dundee in 1908, and up to 1967, they gained a further 30 ships, there being 18 'Cairn' ships and 12 others. In 1928 Furness Withy & Company had purchased Cairns Noble Company Limited, and in 1967 purchased The Cairn Line of Steamships. In effect, the Cairn Line with just over 100 years of trading had owned, acquired, managed, or controlled a total of 85 cargo and cargo liners. During the history of The Cairn Line, there were several changes over the years in restructuring the company regarding "Parent" ownerships, such as: Starks & Cairns; Cairns & Young; Thomas Cairns; Cairns Young & Noble; Cairns Noble; Cairn-Thomson; and The Cairn Line of Steamships. This also includes ships and changes whilst under the ownership of Furness Withy Group.

N.B. There were other shipping companies that sailed the same route from the UK to Canada. Namely:

Aberdeen Atlantic SS Co. (1895–1898) General Cargo and Livestock.

Thomson Line of Dundee (Prior to 1908) General Cargo and Refrigerated Produce.

Ellerman Wilson SS Co. (up to 1966) General Cargo and Flour.

1 FUNNELS & FLAGS

The nomenclature of the Cairn Line's history of funnel and houseflags, contained the colours Red, Black, White and Blue.

Prior to 1883, Thomas Cairns funnel markings were Black with a Red band and White pyramid with a "C" in the middle (F1). No known house flag.

In 1883 Cairns & Young company funnel markings were Black with Red Band and White pyramid with "Y" superimposed on "C" in the middle (F3). The house flag was Red with white pyramid and similar "Y" superimposed on "C" in the middle (HF4).

In 1889 Cairns, Young & Noble company funnel markings were Black with Red band bordered by two White bands and a White pyramid in the middle (F5).

House flag was red with White pyramid in the middle (HF6).

In 1892 Cairn Line of Steamships Company (Cairns, Young & Noble Co.) funnel (F5) and house flag (H6) were kept the same as in 1889.

Prior to 1908, Thomson Line of Dundee's funnel markings were Red with a Black top (F2). House flag was a Blue and White checker, known as the Betsy Norrie (HF8).

In 1908, Cairn-Thomson Line's (Cairns Noble Company) funnel markings were Red with a Black top including two White bands with a White pyramid in the middle (F7). Note: The pyramid shape represents a Scottish Cairn – pile of stones thus a triangle shape. Others believe the pyramid in these markings is said to represent the Great Pyramid of Gizeh, the largest pile of stones, or cairn, in the world.

House flags (already mentioned – HF6 & HF8) were flown at random.

From 1908, the official cap badge was adopted, bearing Gold laurel leaves with crossed flags.

In 1928, the Cairn Line of Steamships Co Ltd (Cairns Noble & Co) funnel and house flags markings were the same as in 1908, namely (F7) [Page 13] & (HF8) [Page 13] – the Blue checked Betsy Norrie becoming the official house flag. During the period of Thomson of Dundee's sailing ships, a lady of this name made a flag of this design and presented one to each new sailing ship.

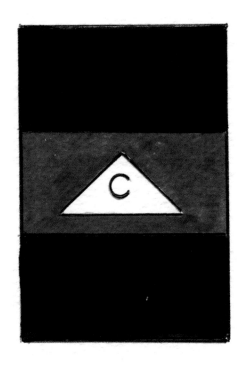

F 1

F 2

F 3

HF 4

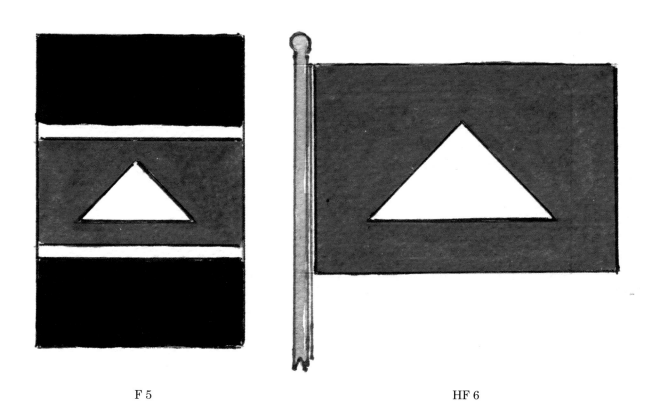

F 5

HF 6

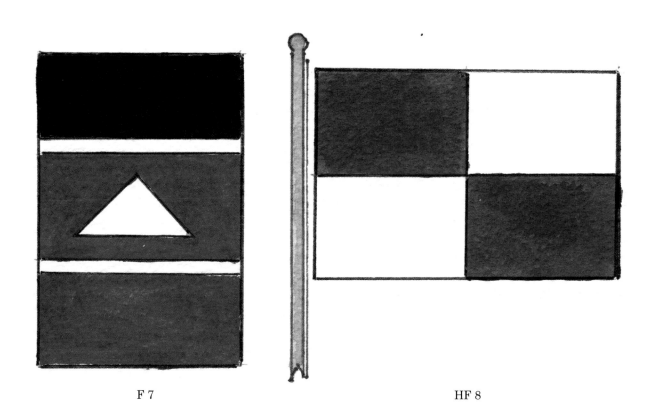

F 7

HF 8

2 THE ROUTES, WEATHER, VOYAGES & TRADE

The Cairn Line of Steamships Co Ltd is known as the shipping company that sailed the Northern Route across the North Atlantic Ocean between the United Kingdom and Canada.

The Cairn Line sailed mainly from Newcastle upon Tyne, Middlesborough on the River Tees, Leith or Grangemouth on the Firth of Forth and from these ports would sail northerly in the North Sea, then westwards through the Pentland Firth and out into the North Atlantic Ocean. Sail onwards south of Iceland and Greenland (not that the author saw these lands like the adventurous Vikings did many, many years ago) and continue southwest heading towards the Island of Newfoundland.

As the Cairn Line navigated the northern trade route, weather forecasts by the Met Office over the BBC shipping forecast service was indeed very important. First introduced by the BBC in 1926, the company was always interested in the shipping areas they passed through e.g. Forth/Tyne, Dogger, Forties, Cromarty, Fair Isle, Hebrides, Bailey/Rockall, sometimes Viking, Faroes and SE Iceland when trying to sail away from very severe weather conditions. In 1853, the Met Office was created by Admiral Robert Fitzroy who was extremely interested and involved in preparing charts of expected weather conditions and gave warnings to shipping. The first barometer was named after the Admiral. There were other broadcasts concerning the Northern Atlantic and Canadian Eastern Seaboard.

One way is by the north of Newfoundland, 'Cape Bauld' through the Strait of Belle Isle or by the southern route round by 'Mistaken Point'. Both routes take you into the Gulf of St Lawrence and then the river to the City of Quebec, Montreal and other ports, namely Trois-Rivieres (Three Rivers), Sorel, Chicoutimi. (Port Alfred) which is situated in the Saquenay river. Also St. John's Newfoundland, and latterly traded into the Great Lakes and occasionaly Hudson Bay; and Sept-Isles (Seven Islands).

CAIRNGLEN (II) – Summer – Montreal

These trips would be the summer trade, and the winter trade would be to Halifax, Nova Scotia and St John New Brunswick. The Cairn Line ships had accommodation (good standard) for up to twelve passengers (Example– see Appendix 2—Sailing Schedule).

CAIRNESK (III) – Winter – North Atlantic – *Alan Fairley*

The Cairn Line in their early days greatly extended their routes of trade as tramp ships to many parts, most of them sailing to the Continent, Mediterranean and Baltic and a few to Canada.

The following are examples:

CAIRNGOWAN (I)	Cronstadt, Sierra Leone, Bilbao, Savona, Natal, and Swinemunde
CAIRNDHU (I)	Palermo, Lisbon, Taganrog North of the Sea of Azov in Russia, Odessa (Russia), Venice, Bilbao and Genoa
CAIRNAVON (I)	Huelva (Spain), Tunis, Antwerpen and Hamburg
CAIRNLOCH	New Orleans
CAIRNESK (I)	Las Palmas, Gulf and Denmark
CAIRNCRAG	Gulf and Pensacola (USA)
CAIRNTORR (I)	Canada and Pensacola
CAIRNBAHN	Baltic and Dakar
SCATWELL	Cuba and Greece
CAIRNDON	Rosario (South America)
CAIRNISLA	Savannah (USA)

The trade between the United Kingdom and Canada varied in commodities and greatly increased over the years, so the following is a fine example of the trade involved:-

WESTWARDS TO CANADA

Cargoes would be coal, steel plates and coils of wire, chemicals e.g. Sulphate, Cyanide and machinery including large dynamos, steel boilers, turbines, flooring, pile bars, tank ammunition, explosives, bricks, motor cars, tractors, rolls of carpet, ship hatches (MacGregor), rope, twine, grindstones, confectionery, whisky and other general cargo. On one occasion, a Bailey bridge (City of Quebec).

EASTWARDS TO UNITED KINGDOM

Cargoes would be grain, flour, wheat, maize, paper pulp, newsprint, oat and cereal foods, canned foods, dairy produce including frozen chips, fruit, maple syrup, aluminium, timbers, zinc, copper, silver, potash and asbestos. On occasions, the deep tanks were filled with linseed oil and hay for race horses!!!

At one time there was no direct trade between North East Scotland and North East England with Canada via the Northern Route but this was to change dramatically over the years during the late 19th Century and early 20th Century.

3 THE HISTORY

The Cairn Line of Steamships Ltd history starts in the late 19th Century. Thomas Cairns was born in 1854 in Sunderland and began his career as a very junior clerk with the Cape of Good Hope Steamship Company. In 1875, he transferred, still as a clerk, to Davidson and Charlton, Newcastle upon Tyne and he became a very articulate and efficient employee. In 1876, Thomas was introduced to a B.B. Starks, Master Mariner who had just started a shipbroker and merchant business in Newcastle. Captain Starks invited Thomas to become a partner, so the proposed company became known as Starks and Cairns and it is thought that this was the initial beginning of the Cairn Line. Their offices were in Mercantile Chambers, Newcastle upon Tyne.

They acted as agents for Thomson Shipping Co, Dundee as far back as 1877 when the Thomson's Steamer, STRATHTAY (I) loaded for Leghorn. In 1880, Starks and Cairns handled the Thomson ship, AVLONA, their first Montreal sailing, and they also acted as agents for ships who engaged in European trade. Starks and Cairns were also into the brokerage business and chartering brokers for other companies.

In 1883, there came a second partnership of Cairns with a Lindsay S.Young. On one/sixty fourth share system, T. Cairns 13, L. Young 12, and Thomsons of Dundee 4, and their first venture was having the CAIRNGOWAN (I) built for them by S.P. Austin, Sunderland, launched in 1883. Their second ship was the CAIRNDHU (I) built in 1886. At this time the principal company was T Cairns, with Cairns & Young as managers, their offices still in Mercantile Chambers.In 1888, Stark retired, his partnership being purchased by W.J. Noble, therefore companies of Starks & Cairns with Cairns &Young, terminated in favour of a new company formed by Thomas Cairns, Lindsay S.Young and Cairn's Brother-in-law, William Joseph Noble (W.J.Noble). The Company commenced trading on 1st January 1889, known as Messrs Cairns, Young & Noble. These three partners had nicknames and were known as follows: Cairns as 'Brains', Young as 'Brass' and Noble as 'Impudence'.

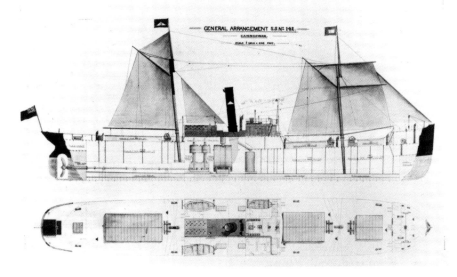

CAIRNGOWAN (I) – *Furness Withy Group*

Again, the new company was owned by the partners on one/sixty fourth share system. Between 1889 and 1902, the principal company was Cairns Young and Noble and along with their subsidiary companies, namely CAIRNGLEN S.S. (1891), CAIRN LINE of S.S (1892), KEROULA S.S. (1895), CAIRNLYON S.S. (1895), and GAELIC S.S. (1898), operated from the Mercantile Chambers (CY&N being managers).During 1892, Cairn Line of Steamships was formed and all new ships completed for them in the future. Up until 1902, there were many transfers of ships between CY&N and their subsidiary companies. In 1897 the above shipping group moved to new offices at Cosyns House, 1-2 Quayside, Newcastle upon Tyne.

In 1902 Lindsay S. Young retired and in 1903, T. Russell Cairns, son of Thomas Cairns, became a new partner, therefore, CY&N was re-styled and became Cairns, Noble & Co. In 1904 Cairn Line of Steamships became the principal company, with Cairns, Noble & Co, as managers. They then opened new offices at 101 Leadenhall Street, London E.C., but retaining Cosyns House as their headquarters, which remained until 1927. During 1904, the CAIRNTORR (I) was launched by W. Doxford & Sons, a turret type ship for Cairns Noble & Co. (the only turret ship ever purchased by the company).

On 24/2/1904, the CAIRNISLA, whilst on a voyage to Canada, came across a ship, MARY A TROOP, which had become damaged and the crew were in great distress after a severe storm.

The Master of the CAIRNISLA, John Oliver Band, went alongside and saved the crew. He was awarded a Silver Cup and an oil painting of the CAIRNISLA with MARY A TROOP in the background, by the Canadian Government, for his bravery. In 1898 Captain Band had joined the Cairn Line as Chief Officer of the CAIRNLOCH. Later, he became Master of the CAIRNGLEN (I), CAIRNISLA (As above), CAIRNTORR (I) and CAIRNGOWAN (II). Captain Band, in common with the other Masters in the company, was expected to 'found' a ship, receiving a fixed sum from the owners to feed the crew. He was a great believer in feeding his crew well, and was rewarded by the fact that crews would willingly wait to 'sign on' with him.

CAIRNISLA – Silver Cup – *John Band*

In 1905, Cairns Noble & Co formed a partnership with Hall Brothers of Cardiff, carrying coke from Germany to Wales, due to a shortage in the Welsh steel works. A company Guest, Keen and Nettlefolds Ltd owners of Dowlais Iron Works ordered a cargo of 7,000 tons of coke from Germany. CAIRNALT shipped in the first cargo of 1,600 tons in April 1905. On 3/9/1908, Thomas Cairns M.P. died. He had been a Liberal M.P. since 1906, and had become an avid opponent of any rules which threatened any British commercial expansion, which led the world, in his day. During 1908, Cairn Line of Steamships acquired the William Thomson Shipping Line of Dundee, and the combined fleets were known as Cairn -Thomson Line. However the Cairn Line of Steamships Co.Ltd now had 25 ships including from Cairns Noble Co, Cairnglen Co and Gaelic Co. Up to 1908, as previously shown, the Canadian routes were added with the acquisition of Thomson Line after 1908.

In time, the company of Cairns Noble were to "spread their wings" and obtain branch offices in London, Cardiff, Middlesborough and Hull, and they also acquired agents in Hamburg and Bremen. Through increasing their trade throughout the UK, they were allocated the following berths for docking to facilitate their cargoes as follows:-

United Kingdom

Aberdeen	Aberdeen Dock
Cardiff	Hall Brothers Company joined with Cairns Noble Company Limited
Dundee	King George V Wharf
Hull	Hull & Barnsley Railway Dock
	In 1906, Cairns Noble, Newcastle, Wm. Brown, Atkinson & Company, Hull and Thomson Line of Dundee registered a company to sail from Hull to Canada. The FREEMONA was the first ship to sail under this arrangement.
Leith	Imperial Dock, Grain Mill (Western Harbour) and Edinburgh Dock.
Middlesborough	Deep Water Wharf
Sunderland	South Dock
Newcastle	Newcastle Quay, Berth No 11 also Dunston Wharf.

Canada

Montreal	No 4 Wharf (was No 11)
Quebec	Quebec Dock
Halifax	Nova Scotia
Saint John	New Brunswick (west side)
St.John's	Newfoundland

U.S.A.

Portland   Maine Grand Trunk Railway Wharf

In the early 19th Century, when a William Thomson (I) Master Mariner from Pittenweem, Fife started up trading with small vessels, principally between Western European ports, Baltic, Norway, Spain and to the Western Mediterranean. In 1829, Captain Thomson and all his crew were lost at sea in the CHRISTIAN, which had been built in 1817, in the port of Dundee.

About thirty years later in 1849, his son William (II) started trading, purchasing the CATHERINE, and in 1850 purchased five more sailing ships.

They were as follows:

NAME	RIG	YEAR BUILT
HEATHER	BRIG	1850
ISIS	BRIG	1850
HELENA	BARQUE	1850
DEODAR	BARQUE	1850
JESSIE	BARQUE	1850

From 1862 William (II) acquired a further 20 sailing ships, several being iron built.

They were as follows:

NAME	SHIP	YEAR BUILT
CANNY SCOT	BARQUE	1862
ARBUTUS	BARQUE	1864
DEODARA	BARQUE	1867-9
BRITISH QUEEN	BARQUE	1867-9
DEODARUS	BARQUE	1867-9
STRATHARDLE	BARQUE	1867-9
FRED THOMSON	BRIG	1867-9
ELIZABETH DOUGALL	BARQUE	1867-9
ROEBUCK	THREE MASTED SCHOONER	1867-9
EUCLID	BARQUE	1870
STRATHEDEN	COMPOSITE BARQUE	1872
ARGUS	BARQUE	1872
REINDEER	BARQUE	1873
LAKE SIMCOE	IRON BARQUE	1873
DUNSINANE	BARQUE	1874
STRATHEARN	IRON BARQUE	1874
CRAIGOWL	BARQUE	1874
DOWNJIEMOUNT	BARQUE	1874
STRATHSPEY	BARQUE	1875
STRATHNAIRN	BARQUE	1876

CANNY SCOT – *D. C. Thomson & Co. Dundee*

SS Gerona of Dundee

GERONA – *D. C. Thomson & Co. Dundee*

BARCELONA – *D. C. Thomson & Co. Dundee*

TORTONA – *D. C. Thomson & Co. Dundee*

His ships continued trading in the Baltic Sea during the time of the Crimean War (1853 – 56). His vessels were also trading to Australia. Later, in 1860, the company traded between UK, Canada and the Mediterranean with larger vessels, becoming known as "The Thomson Clippers". This is believed to be the forerunners of the Thomson Line. In 1871, the steamship STRATHTAY (I), 1,081 GRT was purchased, followed two years later by the steamship SEAGULL. In 1875, the STRATHTAY (I) was wrecked. From then until 1907 more steamships were acquired, replacing the company's sailing ships which were deployed to the Australia and Pacific Coast trade. In turn the steamships were utilised on the Canadian Routes. The Thomson Line Steamships also consisted of the following ships excluding the ships as shown in the aforementioned two ship lists. The ships were the ARONA, CARMONA, DEVONA, GANGES, KILDONA and STRATHTAY (II). The STRATHTAY (II), 1,340 GRT, built 1877 but was wrecked in November of that year. After this incident Thomson's never named another ship – STRATHTAY – I wonder why? As considerable developments were made and with the expansions of steamers, in 1884 William Thomson (II) took on as partners his two elder sons, William (III) and David Couper. His third son Frederick joined in 1888, and the Company became known as Wm. Thomson and Sons. I believe that William (II) was responsible for the commencement of the Thomson Line as he appeared to have the foresight and tenacity to branch out and create trade with other countries, to a larger extent than his father, William (I).

The Thomson Line of Dundee increased in tonnage and eventually his ships sailed a regular service between London and Montreal with the company being credited by being the first to bring in the new innovation of refrigerated cargo from Canada to the United Kingdom and at one time the Thomson Line carried 84% of the Canadian dairy trade to London.

From 1889, Cairns, Young and Noble continued to act as Agents for the Thomson Line of Dundee, at which time the company had six powerful and high classed ships, namely:

GERONA	4600 tons	420 nominal horse power
FREMONA	2922 tons	295 nominal horse power
ESCALONA	3000 tons	210 nominal horse power
DRACONA	3000 tons	200 nominal horse power
BARCELONA	2800 tons	200 nominal horse power
AVLONA	2800 tons	200 nominal horse power

About 1886, William (II) purchased a local Dundee paper, which was called 'The Courier' and dated back approximately 200 years so some believed. Later David Couper Thomson took charge and started up

Cairn-Thomson Line – Crockery – *William Stanley Wilkinson*

as a Newspaper and Periodical publishing business in Glasgow (the following being examples, Sunday Post, Scots Magazine and comics – The Beano etc.) Manchester and London. So now they were involved in shipping and publishing. Up until 1908, the Cairn and Thomson Shipping Lines worked harmoniously together on the same Canadian routes and both Companies shared the transporting of cargo, vending, and brokerage and were also financially involved when in 1908, the Cairn Line acquired the Thomson Line along with its services to Canada and the Mediterranean. To safeguard their ships, officers and crews, etc., Thomson's approached the Cairn Line to take over their shipping company and allow Thomsons to leave their 'money' in the new combined shipping company. This was accepted and Thomsons became investors without control of the new Cairn-Thomson Shipping Company. In 1908 the Thomson Fleet at that time consisted of eight ships, namely and along with particulars of the ship's officers.

BELLONA 2932 GRT

Master, Cunningham, Extra Master's Certificate

Joined October 1893

1st Mate Weschke, Master's Certificate

Joined 1906

2nd Mate F.J. Simpson

CERVONA 3779 GRT

Master. C.T. Stooke Extra Master's Certificate

Joined November 1886

1st Mate M. Johnson Master's Certificate

Joined January 1900

2nd Mate H.J. Broderiak

3rd Mate J.A. Lyles. 2nd Mate's Certificate

Joined 28th February 1908

DEVONA 3779 GRT

Master D.L. Murray, Extra Master's Certificate

Joined 6th June 1892

1st Mate D.A. Laing Master's Certificate

Joined 18th August 1897

2nd Mate A.W. Swapp 1st Mate's Certificate **

Joined February 1907

3rd Mate F. Good 2nd Mate's Certificate

Joined 25th October 1912

** It is believed that this man was also on the CAIRNMONA (II) when she was sunk on 30th October 1939. It is not believed that he got his Master's Certificate. He was apparently quite a character, a smuggler of some sorts, in the times when alcohol was banned in the U.S.A. and when the ships traded to Portland Maine.

FREMONA 2922 GRT

Master D. Ritchie. Extra Master's Certificate

1st Mate W. Thompson

Joined May 1906

2nd Mate J. Laurie

3rd Mate A.J. Moffat

Joined 25 July 1912

HURONA   3432 GRT

Master William Lindsay Master's certificate
1st Mate A.C. Dickson Master's Certificate
Joined 17 June 1905
2nd Mate A. Leask
Joined 12 July 1912
3rd Mate L. Ward
Joined May 1912

IONA   3344 GRT

Master J. Hislop Master's Certificate
Joined August 1892
1st Mate A. Gilbert Master's Certificate
Joined 15th April 1911
2nd Mate F.J. Watts
3rd Mate J.W. Manson

JACONA   2969 GRT

Master S. Grund Extra Master's Certificate
Joined 5th May 1894
1st Mate J. Petrie Master's Certificate
Joined 28th March 1906
2nd Mate J. Johnson Master's Certificate
Joined 26 March 1910
3rd Mate H. Bowles

LATONA   4338 GRT

No record of officers.

A William N Kay sailed as Chief Engineer on a steamer named CELERITY, owned by a company called James Mitchell of Dundee. The CELERITY was lost with all hands in the Baltic Sea in November 1873. One of the lifeboats drifted ashore and in it was one body, which was still warm. This was the only trace of the loss.

The son of the above, also named William N Kay, MBE, served as an engineer with the Thomson Line of Dundee on their ships, namely, CERVONA, ESCALONA, HURONA, FREMONA, LATONA, and the DEVONA.

Later he sailed on the CAIRNMONA (II) from 1918 to 6/11/1935, when he died in mid-Atlantic and was buried at sea.

During 1906 the WARRIGAL (Blue Anchor Line) was sold to Wm Thomson of Dundee and re-named LATONA, and in 1908 sold on to Cairn Line of Steamships. On 20/5 that year the LATONA was sunk in collision with the British ship JAPANIC off the Wolf Rock Lighthouse.

On 21/5/1908 the CONSUELO (Thomas Wilson Son & Co) was sold to Cairn Line of Steamships and re-named CAIRNRONA. On 17/8/1909 the TORTONA was launched, and the GERONA was launched on 6/3/1911. At this time, the Cairn Line was governed by the energetic manner of Sir William Joseph Noble. The company consisted of its highest number of 26 ships with a total tonnage of over 120,000 tons in 1910. However the CAIRNROSS (I) went aground near Tangiers on 5/12/1910 – C.T.L.

The following is an example of ships per annum from 1908 to 1914:-

1908   25 Ships
1909   25 Ships
1910   26 Ships
1911   21 Ships
1912   19 Ships
1913   17 Ships
1914   17 Ships

However, before the completion of the GERONA, along with the CAIRNRONA and TORTONA, these three ships and goodwill of passenger services between the UK and Canada were sold to Cunard Steamship Co. Cunard also acquired a large interest in the Anchor Line (Henderson Bros. Ltd). At the same time the three ships were re-named as follows:-

CAIRNRONA   –   ALBANIA
TORTONA   –   AUSONIA
GERONA   –   ASCANIA

AUSONIA

A point of interest, Charlie Chaplin travelled on the CAIRNRONA on his first voyage to the U.S.A., later becoming a famous film star!

With regard to the TORTONA, she was a four masted passenger and cargo ship, of 7,907 GRT, 8,600 deadweight, twin screw, speed 15 knots. Built for the Cairn-Thomson Line for the immigrant trade between Italy and Canada. It had accommodation for 37 first class and 1,200 immigrants. The tween-deck was insulated to carry perishable cargo being cooled by a cold air system with another tween-deck space cooled by the brine-pipe system. About this time Russell Cairns, son of the founder, and William Black Noble, son of William Joseph Noble joined the Cairn line. In 1912, Cairns Young & Noble Co. ceased trading as shipowners, but were still managers for the Cairn Line of Steamships. Prior to 1912, Keroula Steamship Co. ceased to trade and the following companies ceased trading in 1912, namely Gaelic Steamship Co., Cairnlyon Steamship Co. and Cairnglen Steamship Co. The following ships were built and designed to the same dimensions, having indentical boilers and propellers, namely the CAIRNGOWAN (II), built 1911 with triple expansion engines and the CAIRNROSS (II) with two steam turbines geared to a single shaft. As a result, Mr Charles Waldie Cairns B.Sc. (cousin of Thomas Cairns) prepared and gave a lecture on his paper on the comparative trial results of the two ships, which appeared in the first issue of the "Shipbuilding & Shipping Record" 3/4/1913.

Note: Charles Waldie Cairns B.Sc.

The above was employed as Marine Superintendent for Cairn Steamship Co.for many years.

As early as 1886, submarines had been laid down at Barrow-on-Furness, with no success due to submerging difficulties. Throughout the years there were many amalgamations e.g. Barrow-on-Furness Iron Shipbuilding Co. joined with Nordenfelt Co. and in 1897 Vickers acquired the above along with the Maxim Gun Co. During this period an Irish American, John P. Holland designed a submarine, but still had no success from investors. In 1898, an Isaac L. Rice obtained Holland's designs and took over Holland Torpedo Boat Co., changing the name into the Electric Boat Co.Later, Vickers (Armament & Shipbuilding & Sons, and Maxim Ltd) was awarded a licence to build Holland's submarines, which they did – Holland – Submarines No's 1 to 5 between 2/10/1901 and 10/6/1902. Between 1901 and 1903, Charles Waldie Cairns was believed to have been "headhunted" by Hiram Maxim, Grays Central Machine Engine Works, Barrow-on-Furness to supervise the construction of the five Holland's submarines for the UK. C.W. Cairns returned to Cairns Co. on completion of this work.

Going back to 1910, investigations were made about the feasibility of geared turbines for cargo ships. In 1887, a steamship EASTERN PRINCE 2,147 GRT had been built by Short Brothers of Sunderland for the Prince Steam Shipping Company, engines were triple expansion three cylinder by George Clark of Sunderland. After 1909, two experimental steam turbines, with a geared reduction to a single shaft were built and installed by Parsons Marine Turbine Co. Ltd. In 1909, sold to G. Reid & Co., re-named VESPASION, later sold to Parsons Marine Turbine Co. Ltd.The VESPASION was re-engined to investigate the feasibility of experimental turbine engines, but later was sold to W.J. & W.R.Noble, Newcastle. In 1913, the Cairn Line ordered a new hull from W. Doxford, in which to fit her with turbines, but war intervened, so the order was cancelled. Later the new hull was completed as the LORD BYRON for Greek owners. On the outbreak of WWI, T. Russell Cairns and William Black Noble volunteered and joined the army, as did many more thousands of young men who answered the call of their country. T. Russell Cairns returned home, with the rank of Major, but sadly Lieutenant Noble was killed in France.

LORD BYRON – *National Maritime Museum Greenwich*

On 15/6/1915, the CAIRNMONA (II) was torpedoed off Newcastle, but made port under her own steam. The JACONA was mined on 12/8/1915 off Troup Head, with the loss of 29 lives, and CAIRNSTRATH was torpedoed on 4/8/1917 off Ile de Pilier in the Bay of Biscay, with the loss of Captain Thompson and 21 crew. The FREMONA was torpedoed on 31/7/1917 off Ile de Batz with the loss of 11 crew, and later that year the GEORGIOS ANTIPPA was handed over by the Shipping Controller to Cairns Noble & Co. for management, but in November of the same year, she was torpedoed and sunk 6 miles off the Withernsea Lighthouse (North Sea). Also in 1917, the BORG (Swedish Flag), having been taken over by the Shipping Controller (Prize), and managed by Cairns Noble & Co., was torpedoed and sunk off the Lizard Point. On 15/4/1917 the CAIRNDHU (II), when off Beachy Head, and steaming at 9 knots, was torpedoed amidships on the Port side and began listing to Port. It happened at 2345 hours, and the 3rd Mate took command of a lifeboat with 31 crew. They rowed astern of the ship, when U40 surfaced and asked for details of their vessel. The U-Boat then proceeded towards the CAIRNDHU (II), but returned and rammed the lifeboat, whereby all the crew were thrown into the sea. Later the KULLAERG arrived and picked up 20 survivors, landing them at Portsmouth. The Master and six crew had managed to get away in another lifeboat, and next day landed at Newhaven. The wreck of the CAIRNDHU (II) lies in a depth of 90 feet, heading West to East. It is believed that a howitzer gun and ammunition are still on board, as well as a 4.7 inch stern mounted gun.

At the start of WWI in 1914, Cairn Line of Steamships had a fleet of 17 ships, but by the end of the war had only 9 ships.

The following ships were then sold:-

1918	CAIRNLOCH to Capel Steamship Co.	Re-named CAPELBAY
1919	CAIRNNEVIS to Chr. Salvesen	Re-named TOLSTA
1919	CAIRNAVON (I) to Chr. Salvesen	Re-named SOUTRA

Cairns Noble & Co. had management of the above three ships for some time after their sale.

In 1919 Cairn Line of Steamships remaining vessels were CAIRNDHU (III), CAIRNGOWAN (III), CAIRNMONA (II) & CAIRNVALONA, with the last two Thomson ships, DEVONA & HURONA being sold in 1919.

The Cairn Line of Steamships had become a limited company and re-structured to Cairn Line of Steamships Ltd. in 1915. Later, in 1917 the CAIRNSTRATH was sold to Capel & Co., name unchanged, with Cairns Noble & Co. as managers. In 1918 Cairns Noble & Co. became a limited company, but only until 1922, and during this period, the last of the Thomson ships, as previously mentioned, were sold off. During the post-war years, William Joseph Noble and Major T. Russell Cairns carried on running The Cairn Line of Steamships Ltd. and management of Cairns Noble & Co., and the Cairn Line of Steamships retained their limited liability status in 1922. The CAIRNROSS (II) built 1913 was sunk by a torpedo in 1918, however, she was replaced in 1921, by the CAIRNROSS (III) which is believed to be the first cargo ship to be specifically designed to be powered by geared turbines. The turbines were manufactured by Parson's Marine Steam Turbine Ltd, Newcastle. She was in other respects a conventional cargo ship of her period, her tonnage being 5,494 Gross and a Deadweight of 7,830. The CAIRNROSS (III) proved more economical in fuel consumption at about 15% less than her conventionally engined sister-ship, CAIRNGOWAN (III) built 2 years earlier but with the same hull design powered by triple expansion. The CAIRNROSS (III) machinery weighed about 20 tons less. The CAIRNROSS (III) survived an attack whilst in the Mediterranean, when a torpedo missed her on 30/5/1917. However, she was torpedoed again on 27/5/1918 near the Azores and sank. In 1919 the Shipping Controlller, London took over the TOTMES and appointed as managers, Cairns Noble & Co Ltd.

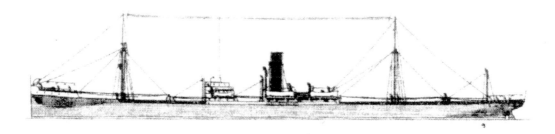

TOTMES – Line Drawing

The Cairn Line lost other ships by enemy action, which were operating under the Government's Liner requisition scheme, known as "The Blue Book Rates" (William Joseph Noble served on this committee).

Apart from ships already mentioned, there were others, namely,
CAIRNGOWAN (II) (1916), CAIRNTORR (I) (1915) and IONA (1915).

On 31/12/1923, the BARQUENTINE 'CZARINA' on voyage from St John's Newfoundland to Pernambuco, Brazil with a cargo of cod fish. When in position, believed to be 46N 51.40W, she got into great difficulties, due to a storm which had been raging for several days in the North Atlantic Ocean. The CZARINA lost her foremast and her main mast had sprung splitting across her midships and she was, with her crew, in a perilous condition.
At this time the CAIRNMONA (II), which was on voyage from the Tyne to Portland Maine, came across the sinking CZARINA whereupon all the crew were saved and taken to Portland.

In the early morning of the 1/11/ 1925, the CAIRNAVON (III) with general cargo of coal, coke, rags and manganese from Leith to Montreal went ashore in dense fog at South Castle Haven (not a very appropriate name) South of a prominent rock called Dundonnie, about a half mile South of Buchan Ness Lighthouse. The fog was so dense, the lighthouse keepers were unaware of the incident until the coastguards arrived looking for the ship. In fact Wick Radio Station had picked up a S.O.S. broadcast from the ship.

It was two hours, because of poor visibility, before the Peterhead Station could locate the CAIRNAVON (III). It became very precarious, that the order to abandon ship was given whereupon the Mate, two crew and one passenger went over the side by a rope ladder onto some rocks. The First Mate and the three others carried torches to find a way off the rocks, up the cliffs. By this time the Coastguards had found the CAIRNAVON (III) and a rope ladder was lowered down the cliff face. It was an extremely difficult operation but 49 crew and passengers were rescued and the CAIRNAVON (III) broke up two days later.

CAIRNAVON (III) – South Castle Haven – *CTL*

In 1926, The Cairn Line issued their accounts for 1924-25-26, showing that the Directors policy had been building up an adequate investments scheme, depending on the necessity of money in the business.In this period, taking into consideration a coal strike, it caused increased working costs, but,the Cairn Line was able to carry on a regular service only by paying double the cost of Canadian bunker coal as compared to the UK price. In doing so, they lost valuable cargo trade (space) on the homeward voyages, however, the increase in profits is attributed to investment income.

The following years are as shown:

Year	Profits	Net Profits	Dividend %	Contingencies	Carried Fwd
1924	£75,331	£57,238	5	£10,000	£18,701
1925	£71,435	£50,224	5	NIL	£20,926
1926	£81,717	£58,896	5	£10,000	£21,821

In the last year, the CAIRNESK (III) and CAIRNGLEN (II) were purchased, which appeared to add to the excellent earnings of the company, thus giving an overall satisfactory improvement.

The fleet now had 9 cargo ships of 46,925 tons, also including all properties, buildings and refrigeration installations, the value on the Company Books read as £1,332,213. This was regarded moderate, allowing for the type of ships involved. They were:

NAME	BUILT	ACQUIRED	GRT
CAIRNMONA (II)	1918		4666
CAIRNVALONA	1918		6402
CAIRNDHU (III)	1919		5230
CAIRNGOWAN (III)	1919		5295
SCATWELL	1911	1919	4425
CAIRNROSS (III)	1920		5494
CAIRNTORR (II)	1922		5387
CAIRNESK (III)	1926		5007
CAIRNGLEN (II)	1926		5019

In 1926, (with the Stock Market Crash not far away), shipbuilding and marine engineering orders were starting to fall off compared to previous years. e.g., companies in Sunderland

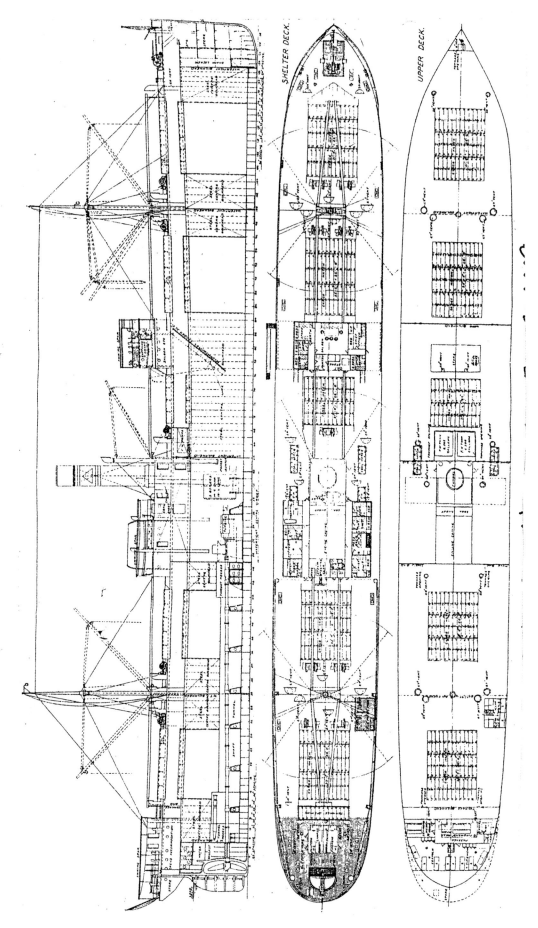

CAIRNROSS (III) – Plan – *National Maritime Museum of Greenwich* – 1920

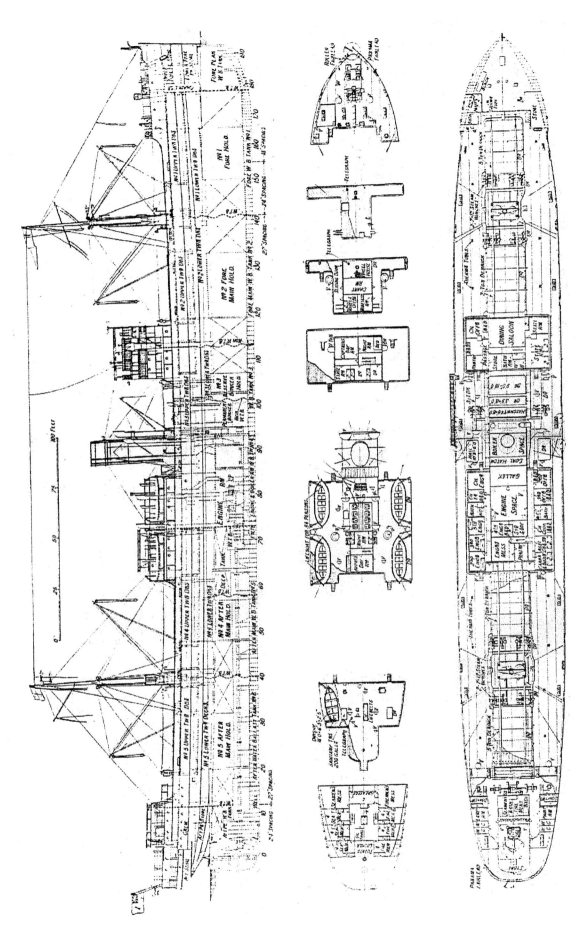

CAIRNESK (III) – Plan – *National Maritime Museum of Greenwich* – 1926

Tonnage

Shipbuilders	1924	1925	1926
Pickersgill & Sons	14,506	12,876	10,026*
Short Bros.	20,108	9,260	7,313
Laing & Sons	18,283	11,609	7,286
Thompson, JL & Sons	18,492	4,677	5,300
Blumer & Co.	Nil	Nil	7,054
Gray, William & Co. (1918)	20,053	16,566	Nil
Thompson, Robert J & Sons	13,260	3,677	Nil
Priestman & Co.	10,115	12,475	—
Crown & Sons	6,161	3,095	Nil
Osbourne, Graham & Co.	2,481	969	Nil
Doxford & Sons	28,074	—	Nil

*Note: The tonnage shown by Pickersgill & Sons in 1926, were the building of CAIRNESK (III) and CAIRNGLEN (II) (sister ships).

Marine Engineering	1924	1925	1926
	IHP	IHP	IHP
Dickinson, John & Sons	18,080	6,850	6,020
Clark, George Ltd.	8,971	8,066	1,500

The same trend was affecting other companies throughout the UK.

In 1927 Cairn Line of Steamships moved from Cosyns House to Akenside House, Newcastle, still having a fleet of 9 ships, previously mentioned. The company only stayed until 1930, when they moved to Milburn House, Newcastle, remaining there until 1970. Also in 1927 there were rumours "flying around" that Cunard Line had purchased Cairn Line of Steamships Ltd, that Canadian Pacific had obtained a controlling interest, and that Furness Withy had acquired the entire Cairn Line of Steamships Ltd.

However, shares in the Newcastle Stock Exchange were active compared to the London stock Exchange. The shares rose from 19/- (95p) to 25/- (£1.25p), but fell back to 23/- (£1.15p). Later in 1928, Furness Withy acquired Cairns Noble & Co., the first company to be taken over by them since WWI. The intention of Furness Withy was to purchase the Cairn Line of Steamships Co. Ltd, but a rise in it's market share price changed Furness's policy to purchase. Instead, Furness Withy bought Cairns Noble Co. Ltd., thus gaining control of the of the Cairn Line fleet. The price for the £50,000 capital of Cairns Noble Co. Ltd. was £267,500, the bulk of which was in Furness Withy shares, £220,000. It was considered a good purchase with a possible profit return of about £40,000 to £50,000 per annum, and in exchange, 50,000 Cairn Line shares were purchased from Sir William Noble for 25,000 Furness Withy shares.

The senior partner, Sir William J Noble was rewarded for his services to shipping and his country, by being made a Baronet in 1920, becoming Baron Kirkley of Kirkley, Northumberland. Lord Kirkley bought Kirkley Hall near Ponteland North West of Newcastle upon Tyne from the Ogle family in 1922. He retired from the Newcastle office and became a director of Furness Withy in 1930. Lord Kirkley died on 11/9/1935 at the age of 72. It would be remiss not to give a resume of Lord Kirkley's achievements. He appeared to be a man of vision, enterprise, believed in good education for further advancement of the commercial and industrial life of the country. He was born on the 13/1/1863 in Newcastle and educated at his father's academy (John Noble) William Noble's first appointment at fourteen years was with Messrs Stephens Kindrick & Mawson, ship owners and brokers. On 12th March 1877, this firm was under the title of Stephen Sutton Ltd. He quickly moved on to management with Messrs Chapman and Miller. Later when 25 years old, he went into partnership with Thomas Cairns, resulting in the formation of the Cairn Line of Steamships in 1892. Lord Kirkley became president of the Chambers of Shipping of the United Kingdom, also president of the Baltic and White Sea Conference (International Body). In 1919, he became president of the Institute of Chartered Ship Brokers and also elected to head the Economic Mission, visiting South Africa with a view to prospects to trading. Lord Kirkley then became chairman of Tyne Improvement Commission for five years until 1930.He also became the first president of the Newcastle Shipbrokers Association and also involved with Newcastle and Gateshead Chamber of Commerce. Not forgetting that in 1921, he became president of the North East Coast Institution of Engineers and Shipbuilders. Lord Kirkley was actively involved with many other committees and associations including during World War I starting three scholarships with the Faculty of Commerce at the Armstrong College, Newcastle.

On 12/3/1927, he celebrated his business jubilee.

Lord Kirkley of Kirkley

On 23/10/1928, the CAIRNTORR (II) was wrecked on Island Rock, Cocoacho, Labrador Coast, whilst failing to clear the estuary. The crew got two boats away and were later rescued by Donaldson Line's SALACIA. By the end of the month, the CAIRNTORR (II) broke up and sank, in position 50.7 N 60.17W. In 1929, the CAIRNGOWAN (III), under the command of Captain F.W. Fairley, whilst on passage from UK to Canada, lost her rudder. A jury rudder was rigged and the ship sailed over 500 miles until they encountered ice. As they approached St John's, Newfoundland, the s.s. HUMBER towed the CAIRNGOWAN (III), and the tugs MOHTON and HUGH D came out to assist with the towage. Also in attendance was the CAIRNDHU (III).

Having moved to Milburn House in 1930, Cairns Noble & Co. became the principal company with Cairn Line of Steamships Ltd retained as the management company. They also changed their previous London address to 38 St Helens Street, EC3.

During the depression throughout the 1930's, after the Stock Market Crash in 1929, unemployment was very high, reaching approximately 3 million in 1932/33.

Unemployment was "right across the board" in most industries, including the British Mercantile Marine. Ships of all types were laid up all over the UK, due to the fall in trading (some companies never recovered from the collapse).

In 1931, Cairn Line had 7 ships, CAIRNESK (III), CAIRNGLEN (II), CAIRNROSS (III), and CAIRNVALONA continuing to trade. The CAIRNGOWAN (III) traded for 4 months, but joined the CAIRNDHU (III) laid up on the Tyne in 1930.

The CAIRNMONA (II) was laid up in Blyth. The CAIRNGOWAN (III) and CAIRNDHU (III) were sold off in 1935.

The following number of idle ships varied greatly in different locations. For example, in 1933:-

ENGLAND

Tees	3 Ships	
Sunderland	26 Ships	
Tyne	88 Ships	(Approximate)
Blyth	12 Ships	

SCOTLAND

Leith	5 Ships
Grangemouth	9 Ships

To realise the number of crew unemployed in these 6 locations, multiply each ship with an average of crew of 40, it comes to quite a total – over 5,500. All told, there were 46 places (including the above) in the UK, the end result of unemployment in the Merchant Navy was colossal, to say the least.

On 23/3/1934, the CAIRNGLEN (II) ran ashore on a reef on the Huna Harbour in Caithness when eastbound through the Inner Sound between the Isle of Stroma and St John's Point. It happened at low tide, so tenders came alongside and cargo was removed to lighten the ship. CAIRNGLEN (II) had been carrying general cargo from Halifax, Nova Scotia to Newcastle.

When tide was high, the tug SEAMAN towed her off and took the CAIRNGLEN (II) to Lyness, and then onto the Tyne where repairs had to be made to her boilers and turbines, which had been displaced. The CAIRNGLEN (II) was taken to the Middle Docks and Engineers Co., in South Shields. The CAIRNGLEN (II) was a special heavily constructed ship and had a deck liner fixed to every frame, and stiffened for ice protection. The following structures were renewed:

The tank top plates of the engines, boilers of number two hold, the bottom shell plating and the double bottom tank internal structure. The Parson's turbines and the three boilers were removed to allow this work to be carried out, the whole operation being completed in four months.

Note: The SEAMAN, built 1924, steel screw tug, O.N. 148409, (Yard No. 943), 369 Tons, 125' x 28' x 14'6", 1050 (NHP) Nominal Horse Power, by Earles Shipbuilding & Engineering Co, (Cochranes of Selby), cost £16,300, for United Towing Company of Hull. The SEAMAN had a flying bridge with wheelhouse and fitted with wireless telegraphy.

CAIRNGLEN (II) – Aground on reef – *Alan Fairley*

On the 16th November 1935, the following Steam Trawlers were berthed in North Shields.

The DORILEEN from Aberdeen was lying moored along side the THOMAS W IRVINE from North Shields at Number 2 Tier. Also the WILLIAM HALLETT from London and the AGNES H HASTIE from North Shields were moored alongside the Fish Quay.

At 1655 hours the same day the CAIRNMONA (II) was sailing westwards up the Tyne River. When opposite North Shields and close to Number 2 Tier, the CAIRNMONA (II) sheered northwards, whereby her starboard side collided with and damaged the DORILEEN A412. Both the DORILEEN and the THOMAS W IRVINE broke free and drifted inshore alongside the AGNES H HASTIE.To prevent the DORILEEN sinking in the Channel, the steam tug, HENDON took her in tow to Bill Quay and beached her seventy feet from Messrs Harrison and Robinson's Quay. In the collision the CAIRNMONA (II) also fouled four buoys, after which she was taken in tow by the steam tugs, GEORGE V WASHINGTON and JOSEPH CROSTHWAITE and taken up river. The THOMAS W IRVINE was re-moored and the DORILEEN was later re-floated and taken to a dry dock owned by Shields Engineering and Dry Dock Company. CAIRNMONA (II) was held responsible and damage to one of the buoys estimated at sixteen pounds, any other damage unknown.

DORILEEN – Steam trawler – Beached

At the outbreak of WW II in 1939, Cairns Noble & Co. had 5 ships:-
CAIRNESK (III), CAIRNGLEN (II), CAIRNROSS (III), CAIRNMONA (II) and CAIRNVALONA. New tonnage had been arranged, in fact an order for a ship, proposed name CAIRNFORTH, but was cancelled on the outbreak of hostilities. However, the order was taken over and commissioned by the Prince Line as the WELSH PRINCE. On 7/12/1941 the WELSH PRINCE was sunk by an acoustic mine off Spurn Point, entrance to River Humber. No lives were lost.

On 17/10/1939 the CAIRNMONA (II), along with 15 other ships in Convoy HX5B, sailed from Montreal/ Halifax to Leith & the Tyne, her cargo was grain & copper. Later on, 30/10/1939, the CAIRNMONA (II) was torpedoed and sunk by U13 (Daublebsky Von Eichman) one of the small coastal submarines off Peterhead, Position 49.57N 07.37W – 3 lives were lost. The Master, Captain Fred Fairley and 41 crew were rescued by HMS RIVER LOSSIE, built 1920, Captain J.C. Spence, RNR.

In January 1940, U30 Commander Fritz Lemp laid several mines in the Irish Sea near the entrance to the River Mersey, which made it particularly dangerous to shipping. (Lemp was responsible for the sinking of the ATHENIA, built 1923, being the first casualty of WWII, when torpedoed by U30 to the west of Inishtrahull, Ireland). On 6/1/1940, the CAIRNROSS (III), with 18 other ships forming Convoy OB74, were sailing outwards, bound from Liverpool to St John N.B. The CAIRNROSS (III) had already called at

Leith and the Tyne, her cargo consisted of coal, earthenware and general cargo. Approximately 8 miles from the Mersey Bar L.V., she struck a mine and sank. The Captain and 47 crew were rescued.

In 1940, The EMPIRE SNOW, was built in Glasgow for the Ministry of War Transport under the Tonnage Replacement Scheme. In 1941 this vessel was handed over to Cairns Noble for management. They later purchased the ship in 1946 and re-named her CAIRNAVON (IV).

Note: The Chief Officer of the EMPIRE SNOW, Ian Grant Foster, whilst sailing in the Russian Convoys, twice received an award for bravery, first as Chief Officer on board the WHITECREST – Commended for Bravery. Secondly as Chief Officer on the EMPIRE SNOW – Mentioned in Dispatches. Later he served as Master on both CAIRNESK (III) and CAIRNGOWAN (IV).

In 1940, Cairns Noble Co Ltd took management of a prize of war, from the Royal Navy, namely: EMPIRE BRIGADE ex ELIOS, built 1912, 5,154 GRT. On 18/10/1940 this ship was torpedoed by U99 (Kretschmer) to the West of St Kilda.

Prior to this incident, the EMPIRE BRIGADE had sailed from the UK to Canada, but unfortunately lost her convoy, and making her own way over, she encountered a U-Boat on the surface. It was bad weather, but never the less both were surprised to see one another. Both fired a shell at each other before the bad weather took over completely. The U-Boat's shell missed the EMPIRE BRIGADE, but the bad weather was so severe that her centre-castle was shifted back five inches. She needed substantial repairs in Halifax N.S. before she could join Convoy SC7 for the homeward passage. Her cargo on this voyage consisted of 7,000 tons of copper ore, 3,000 tons of grain, large quantities of tinned foods. In addition, she had 18 Army Lorries secured on the after deck.

Back to 5/10/1940, the EMPIRE BRIGADE had joined Convoy SC7, and along with another 34 ships had departed from Sydney, Cape Breton for the UK. This convoy was regarded to be slow, most ships sailing at 7/8 knots. On 18/10/1940 a German Wolf Pack of 5 U-Boats attacked the convoy and started to decimate it with ferocious intent, to the degree that in 24 hours, 20 ships had been torpedoed and sunk, with many lives lost. This attack in credited as being the first of U-Boats combining together and acting as a "force" instead of operating alone, and it appears to have been very successful. Other convoys were to meet the same treatment, e.g. PQ17, HX71, ON127, SL7, SC167 to name but a few. There were approximately 500 convoys during World War II.

The EMPIRE BRIGADE was hit with a torpedo on the Starboard side amidships, the First Radio Officer, Leonard Dewar immediately sent out a message "No 53, torpedoed starboard side" and then raced to the bridge, where Captain Parkes, on assessing the damage, believed EMPIRE BRIGADE had no hope of staying afloat. He then gave the order to abandon ship, so Captain Parkes and his Officers went to the boat deck, to find that all the boats had already been launched. None of the crew had waited for the order to abandon ship, whereupon the Master and his Officers jumped into the sea. They were then picked up by their own lifeboats.

The EMPIRE BRIGADE was still steaming ahead, with the propeller racing. The engine room and holds filled up with sea water and the ship disappeared bow first less than 50 seconds later.

Captain Sydney Wyman Parkes and 34 crew were rescued by HMS FOWEY, a Sloop built in 1930, 1,105 GRT (L15), Lt Commander C.G. de L. Bush, and later landed at Greenock.

On 22/10 of the same year, 1940, the CAIRNGLEN (II) was wrecked off Marsden, South Shields. This incident appears rather tragic to a degree, the circumstances were as follows:-

On 22nd October 1940, the Captain of the CAIRNGLEN (II) had sighted a black/white buoy, laid by a minesweeper the previous day. This marked the southern channel up the coast thereby leading into the Tyne. But it was mistaken for a buoy leading straight into the estuary. The CAIRNGLEN (II) turned to starboard but went aground for approximately 400 feet. This sheared her propeller and she was unable to go astern. There was a heavy fog along the coast and her cargo contained railway line, trucks, food, including bacon. As the Captain saw the black and white buoy thought he was safe and turned to starboard. This new direction took the ship straight onto inshore reefs and the weather worsened. The weather conditions were stormy and very broken sea and impossible to launch any lifeboats. The crew took station at the stern, and the Sunderland and Roker Rocket Brigade were notified at 0500 hours but they thought the wreck appeared to be too far off shore. The CAIRNGLEN (III) drifted and by 1900 hours came within reach of the shore, then broke her back.

By now, her crew got out the lifeboats and about 20 members reached the beach. Later the rest of the crew who had stayed onboard were saved when a William Burton was sent across by bosun's chair and he persuaded them to leave the ship. Mr Burton received the B.E.M. for his bravery. Much of the general cargo was retrieved by breeches buoy and when Winston Churchill was informed of the incident he commended them for "saving our country's bacon".

The Cairn Line was managing the BLACK OSPREY, ex WAR ARROW on behalf of the Ministry of Transport, the ship having been recently purchased by the British Government. The BLACK OSPREY had been one of the American owned ships built for the American Black Diamond Line at the end of World War I and sold to the UK. Another ship was the BLACK ARROW, but was lost before being renamed as an Empire ship. Only four months later on 18/2/1941, the BLACK OSPREY was torpedoed by U96 (Lelmann-Willenbrook), south of Iceland, position 61.30N 18.10W whilst a straggler from convoy HX107 comprising of 21 ships. They were on voyage from Baltimore, Newport via Halifax, N.S. and the BLACK OSPREY was carrying a cargo of 4,500 tons of steel and trucks, sad to say that Sydney Wyman Parkes, Master Mariner and twenty four crew were lost. Eleven crew members rescued by U96 (Korvettenkapitan Heinrich Lelmann-Willenbrook) (Knights Cross 26/2/1941 with Oak Leaves on the 31/12/1941). The crew transferred to the Norwegian ship, MOSSDALE, built 1939, 3,022 GRT, landed at Barry Roads. The statistics for the month of October 1940 recorded the highest tonnage of 352,407 tons sunk by the U-boats. There were 63 merchant ships lost, almost a third of these from one Convoy, SC7. Between July and October 1940, it was a peak achievement by the Germans, which their U.B. commanders called 'the happy time'.

A third ship, the EMPIRE LAPWING, ex BLACK CONDOR, built 1921, was later transferred from the Cairn Line to the Belgian flag, but shortly afterwards was sunk by a U-Boat.

On the 13th May 1941, in convoy W8 six ships were lost and up to the end of May of that year although thirty one UB's were destroyed, the U.K. and allies lost 882 ships. Sometime later the USN REUBEN JAMES was torpedoed with a loss of 115 personnel. By December 1941 Pearl Harbour was attacked and the U.S.A. came into World War II.

The following is an example of UB's moving in for the 'kill' second time around. The EMPIRE SUNRISE (not managed by Cairns Noble & Co.) was hit twice within 3 hours; however the following paragraph shows the sterling work carried out by rescue ships as follows;

On the 2nd November 1942 at 0205 hours, Convoy SC107 was in position 51.50N 46.25W, approximately 500 miles east of Belle Isle. The EMPIRE SUNRISE was torpedoed by U402 (Lt/Commander Siegfried V. Forstner). She received one hit but did not sink. Later at 0521 hours the same day the EMPIRE SUNRISE was given the 'Coupe de Grace' by U84 (Lt Horst Uphoff). All the crew were saved being picked up the rescue ship, STOCKPORT, eventually landing in Reykjavik. The STOCKPORT saved 149 Merchant Navy personnel from the ships sunk in that Convoy. The accompanying tugs, the UNCAS and PESSACUS assisted the STOCKPORT and between them saved 240 seaman during the attack.

In 1942, Cairns Noble & Co took over management of another prize (Italian) from the RN.

m.v. EMPIRE SAILOR, ex CELLINA, built 1926, 7,061 GRT was torpedoed on 21/11/1942 at 0030 hours by U518 (Wissmann) whilst on passage from Liverpool to St John NB in Convoy ON145, comprising 35 ships. Included in the EMPIRE SAILOR's cargo were some 430 tons of toxic materials, including 270 tons of phosgene gas, 26 tons of mustard gas in 68 drums, and also ammunition in the form of five inch rocket shells. A torpedo struck the ship, causing cyanide gas to escape engulfing the ship. Captain Fred Fairley, Master of the vessel ordered an immediate abandonment due to the concentration of the gas, so the crew took to the lifeboats (Captain Fairley was in command of the CAIRNMONA (II) when torpedoed in 1939).

The crew were picked up by HMCS MINAS, a minesweeper of the Canadian escort and HMCS TIMMINS, a corvette. The survivors symptoms puzzled their rescuers, but a Surgeon Lt Slessor was transferred from HMS WANDERER to attend these men. The surgeon recognised the symptoms and it was confirmed by Captain Fairley who advised Lt Slessor as to the nature of the cargo.

The following is an example of personnel numbers of survivors, and those lost in a sinking. In this case it is the m.v. EMPIRE SAILOR. Some ships did not lose as many men, but many other vessels lost more men, and sometimes entire crews.

EMPIRE SAILOR – *Alan Fairley*

M.V. EMPIRE SAILOR torpedoed 21st November 1942
Details of crew survivors and those who were lost:

	Survived	Lost	Total
Master	1		1
Deck Officers	3		3
Cadets	3		3
Radio Officers	3		3
Engineers	7	2	9
Bosun		1	1
Carpenter		1	1
Electricians	2		2
Storekeeper	1		1
Donkeyman/greaser	1	6	7
A.B.'s	4	6	10
Catering	8	4	12
Merchant Navy Crew	**33**	**20**	**53**
R.N. Gunners	2	3	5
R.C.N.V.R. Signalmen	2		2
Army Personnel	3		3
Total	**40**	**23**	**63**

N.B. 3 men were missing presumed drowned, 18 men died on board the rescue craft due to gas inhalation and a further 2 died in Halifax.

Note: In the Second World War, ships were bringing metal scrap for the War effort, it was worked out that one ton of scrap was used for the following items:

One 75 mill. field gun; Twelve machine guns; One 16 inch battleship piercing shell or Nine 500 pound bombs. Also in the first convoy to the U.K. part of ships cargoes were one million feet of fire hose.

In 1943 the CAIRNVALONA, whilst in convoy ON176, was in collision with a Norwegian manned four stack British destroyer, HMS BEVERLEY which caused heavy damage to that vessels sonar. As a result the HMS BEVERLEY could not hear and could only make 15 knots, she was therefore vulnerable and was attacked and sunk by U188, only 4 of her crew of 152 were saved.

In 9/1946, the CAIRNVALONA was on a voyage from Newcastle to Montreal. Whilst passing the Anticosti Isle in the St Lawrence, the Chief Engineer Arnold Williamson, became aware that the bearings were becoming warm.

It was seen that circulating water intake pipe to engines were not circulating the required amount of water to cool the engines. It was discovered that her circulating pipes were crammed with fish. Seafarers knew them to be the sailor's choice or Bream (proper name). During the time the pipes were cleared, the CAIRNVALONA drifted in the current. The engineers cleared the fish away in two hours. The Bream are slim fish about six inches long and the CAIRNVALONA had sailed through a shoal, sucking them into the pipes. On the homeward voyage the CAIRNVALONA called into St John's Newfoundland and loaded cargo of 1,250 of frozen fish for Newcastle (the last laugh).

CAIRNVALONA – Quayside, Newcastle – *Marion Foster*

On 22/5/1945, U518 commanded by Oberleutnant Zur Hans Offerman and with 55 crew were lost when this U-Boat, which was part of a Wolf Pack of 6 U-Boats, was sunk 390 miles NW of Flores, Azores, by U.S. Destroyer escorts in position 43.26N 38.23W. These destroyers were USS CARTER built 1944 1240GRT (DE112) Lt.Commander E.J.T. Baker USS NEAL A SCOTT built 1944 1240GRT (DE769) Lt. Commander P.D. Holden which were part of Task Group 22.5 (Re U518 see EMPIRE SAILOR).

CAIRNGOWAN (IV) – Short Funnel – *William Stanley Wilkinson*

In 1946 Cairns Noble & Co had three ships left, CAIRNESK (III), CAIRNVALONA and the CAIRNAVON (IV) ex EMPIRE SNOW and the company remained like this until 1952. Cairn Line of Steamships Ltd. reverted back as the principal company and Cairns Noble & Co. to managers in 1950. In 1952, Cairn Line of Steamships Ltd. commissioned two new ships, both built by William Gray & Co., namely CAIRNGOWAN (IV) & CAIRNDHU (IV). Note: Dhu, from the Gaelic, means Black, thus CAIRNDHU = Black Cairn. On 30/6/1952, the CAIRNVALONA was sold for scrap to BISCO, allocated to Clayton & Davie, Dunston, it should be noted that she had completed 180 round trips between the UK and Canada.

In 3/1952, a local photographer took a photo of The CAIRNESK (III) in its usual berth in Halifax N.S. A liberty ship, KYLE V JOHNSON was berthed opposite. The ship in middle background was the CANADIAN CHALLENGER, it was a C3-5-A3 type vessel built as a troop ship. After WWII converted into a passenger ship.

CAIRNESK (III); KYLE V JOHNSON – Halifax N.S. – *Maritime Museum of the Atlantic, Nova Scotia, Canada*

On 12/1/1953, The CAIRNESK (III) whilst berthing in St. John N.B., was in collision with the NOVAPORT (already berthed). The CAIRNESK (III) had starboard hawse pipe broken and shell plate in way torn. The NOVAPORT had one shell plate very slightly indented and minor damage to port bridge wing. *(Lloyds Weekly Casualty Reports 20/1/1953)* The CAIRNESK (III) sold in 1956, and after a couple of name changes, sailed in 1959 to Japan and was broken up, again, it should be noted that she had completed 204 round trips between the UK & Canada.

In 1958, the CAIRNFORTH was built and completed by Burntisland Shipbuilders Co Ltd (North Shore, Firth of Forth – Opposite Port of Leith). The engines were by Hawthorn Leslie & Co. Between 1959 and 1963 CAIRNFORTH became surplus to the Canadian Trade and was chartered out as follows:-

In 1959 CAIRNFORTH sailed to the Mediterranean & India. Then in 1960 was chartered by the Chinese Government, trading between Shanghai, Hamburg & Liverpool. She was later chartered by Manchester Liners trading to the Eastern seaboard of the USA. Again, the same year, chartered by Elder Dempster Lines of Liverpool and trading to West Africa.

In 1961 chartered to Bank Line, trading to Gulf of Mexico, Makatea and New Zealand (Phospates). In 1962 chartered to Shaw Savill & Albion, trading from London to New Zealand & to Makatea (Phosphates). Later to Queensland, Australia, for a cargo of sugar, and back to Liverpool, and in 1963 resumed the Canadian run.

CAIRNFORTH – On trial, Firth of Forth – *Trinity House Leith*

At the beginning, the Cairn Line had "Trampships", which sailed all over the world. Later in their history, they sailed on regular voyages from the UK to the Eastern Seaboard of Canada. At the end, the CAIRNFORTH (although be it on charter to other companies) sailed as a "Trampship", thus completing the full circle of/for the Cairn Line.

The Cairn Line was not wholly owned by Furness Withy until 1967, but was group controlled, and managed by Cairns, Noble, & Co Ltd. In 1965, the last three cargo-passenger ships of the Cairn Line of Steamships Co Ltd were chartered to Manchester Liners Ltd by Furness Withy Co as follows:

NB Manchester Liners were also part of the Furness Withy "Empire".
1.   CAIRNGOWAN (IV) renamed MANCHESTER ENGINEER (III)
2.   CAIRNDHU (IV) renamed MANCHESTER EXPORTER (II)
3.   CAIRNFORTH renamed MANCHESTER FREIGHTER

MANCHESTER ENGINEER (III) – *Furness Withy Group*

MANCHESTER EXPORTER (II) – *Furness Withy Group*

MANCHESTER FREIGHTER – *Furness Withy Group*

In 1965 CAIRNDHU (IV) was sold to Manchester Liners. In 1967 MANCHESTER ENGINEER (III) reverted back to CAIRNGOWAN (IV) on end of charter, and the MANCHESTER FREIGHTER reverted back to CAIRNFORTH on end of charter. During 1965, Furness Withy chartered two ships from Manchester Liners Ltd to the Cairn Line of Steamships Co for one year before taking them back and both were sold to foreign shipping companies in 1969, as follows:

MANCHESTER FAITH (I) renamed CAIRNESK (IV)

MANCHESTER FAME (I) renamed CAIRNGLEN (III)

MANCHESTER FAITH (I) – *Furness Withy Group*

MANCHESTER FAME (I) – *Furness Withy Group*

In 1965, a ship SCHIAFFINO FRERES, ex APSARA was purchased by the Furness Group, and was renamed CAIRNAVON (V), but re-sold within a year. (See Crew List for 1965 Appendix 1). The CAIRNESK (IV), CAIRNGLEN (III) and CAIRNAVON (V) were used for the Canadian service in the summer of 1965 (See sailing schedule, Cairn-Thomson Appendix 2).

By this time, Cairn Line of Steamships Ltd. was in decline (See abstract of financial returns for the period 1955-1965 Appendix 3). In 1965 Furness Withy acquired the share capital of the Royal Mail Lines, which they already owned, Shaw Savill & Albion Ltd. thus forming the largest shipping group in the British Register. The end of The Cairn Line of Steamships Co Ltd came about, in 1967 when Furness Withy, who already owned Cairns Noble & Co., made an offer to obtain the final 85% of shares held by The Cairn Line of Steamships Co. Ltd., with the overall aim of controlling all North Atlantic services, thus combining all for the Furness Withy Group.

So finally Furness Withy & Co Ltd acquired and wholly owned the Cairn Line of Steamships Co Ltd., who then became a wholly owned subsidiary, with Cairns Noble & Co. as managers, until 1969, when Cairn Line of Steamships Ltd was placed under Shaw Savill & Albion's management control as was the Prince Line. This enabled Shaw Savill & Albion to operate the new fleet of 'Mini-Bulkers', plus the CEDRIC, CANOPIC, IONIC and LINDFIELD. In fact, Shaw Savill & Albion controlled 29 ships in its fleet, plus the ten Cairn Line ships to its management.

The Cairn Line nomenclature was kept for use by the 'mini-bulkers' commissioned by the Group and sometime later in the 1970's the Cairn Line operated from London. The first mini-bulk ship was the CAIRNVENTURE, 2,750 DWT, in 1969, launched by E.J. Smit en Zoon in Holland and delivered to the Cairn Line, which was now a subsidiary of Shaw, Savill & Albion Co Ltd. The CAIRNVENTURE was later sold in 1974 to Shipmair N.V. Rotterdam and renamed SHIPMAIR III. The CANOPIC, CEDRIC and IONIC were transferred to the Cairn Line of Steamships Co Ltd in 1969 and operated until 1973, when they were returned to Shaw, Savill & Albion Co Ltd.

CAIRNTRADER – Launch

In 1971, the following ships were delivered to the Cairn Line of Steamships Co namely the CAIRNRANGER. In the same year, two Prince Line ships, built by Dutch shipbuilders, namely the SAXON PRINCE and PENNINE PRINCE. The SAXON PRINCE had been proposed as the CAIRNTRADER (However, in 1975, the ship was returned and re-named CAIRNTRADER.) The CAIRNROVER in 1972; the CAIRNLEADER and CAIRNFREIGHTER in 1975. In 1976 the CAIRNCARRIER, and in 1977, CAIRNASH, CAIRNELM and CAIRNOAK.

Note: In September 1979, the CAIRNOAK, whilst berthed in Liverpool, was observed flying the houseflag HF6 (As shown in 1889 & 1892. The flag ceased to be flown after 1908).

The last three ships were built in Gdansk Shipyard, the first, and only Polish built vessels for Furness

CAIRNASH – Launch – Gdansk Shipyard

Withy Group. There was a fourth ship proposed as CAIRNLINER, built by Martin Jansen, West Germany, but launched as the BREEZAND (Dutch Flag).

BREEZAND (proposed as CAIRNLINER) – *World Ship Society*

The Mini-Bulk cargo ships under the Cairn nomenclature, all now registered and operated from offices at 14/19 Leadenhall Street, London EC3. The Prince Line was also involved in this transaction of events, all ships mentioned managed by Shaw Savill & Albion. Cairn Line of Steamships also acquired, a ship named LINDFIELD, ex CAP MELVILLE, sold to 'K' Lines Steam Ship Co (Kaye & Son) and re-named LIMPSFIELD in 1973.

In 1971 Brantford Holdings Ltd was formed, to incorporate all the numerous UK offices within the Furness Withy/Houlder Bros. Group. This company began operating in 1972 as Furness, Houlder Shipping, and with Brantford Holdings Ltd. as a subsidiary company. During 1975 Furness Withy interest spread beween Prince Line, Royal Mail Lines, Cairn Line and Dee Navigation, the latter being a four ship company formed to operate in South East Asia and Australian waters (renaming of The Empire Transport Co Ltd).

In 1977 this operation unified everything into a single structure management company, renamed Furness Withy (General Shipping) Ltd. In 1979, Cairn Line of Steamships Co Ltd was restyled into Furness Withy (Shipping) Ltd. On 30 September 1980 the Furness Withy Group was acquired by C.Y. Tung, Hong Kong. However, sadly in 1982 C.Y. Tung died. Later in 1983 the last three ships (Mini-bulkers) under Cairn Line's nomenclature, namely CAIRNASH, CAIRNELM, and CAIRNOAK, were sold to Peter Cremer Co of Singapore. In 1987 the Furness Withy head office moved from London to Redhill, Surrey (as it is today). On 17 October 1990, C.Y. Tung sold most of the Furness Withy Group for £130 million to Rudolf A. Oeter Group & Hamburg-Sudamerkanische D.G. Eggert & Amsinck, through Shaw, Savill (Holdings) Ltd.

Sadly and rather quietly, Furness Withy & Company Limited (formerly Cairn Line of Steamships Co Ltd) was placed into members voluntary liquidation on 15th March 2005, after 113 glorious years of transporting cargoes across the world. The central businesses of the company had long since ceased and the end was thus inevitable.

4 FLEET LIST OF CAIRN LINE

1. CAIRNGOWAN (I) (1883-1909)
O.N. 88733   1286 g. 827 n.   225.4 x 34 x 16.3 feet
Compound 2 cylinders (28½" x 53" x 33") engine, by Blair & Co. Stockton 99.hp.

9/6/1883 Launched by S.P. Austin & Son, Sunderland (Yard No.142) for T. Cairns of Newcastle. Completed 7/1883.
1889 Company restyled Cairns & Young, Newcastle.
1891 Company restyled Cairns, Young & Noble, Newcastle.
3/1900 On fire whilst berthed in London, cabins, saloon, charthouse, bridge all destroyed.
1903 Company restyled Cairns Noble & Co.
30/5/1905 Ashore at Algeciras on voyage Newport (Mon) to Gibraltar. Refloated.
1909 sold to AB J.N. Sanne, Uddevalla, Sweden and renamed ODENSVOLD.
19/3/1918 renamed ODDEVOLD by the same owner.
1927 sold to Rederi A.B. Oddevold (Oscar A. Paborn, managers) Solvesborg, Sweden, without name change.
1938 sold to J. Schander (Ingolf Schander managers), Sweden same name.
28/11/1941. On voyage from Gavle to Holtenau, with a cargo of iron ore, sunk after a collision with the Swedish steamer KATTEGAT. 3 crew members lost their lives. She was later refloated and repaired.
26/8/1950 sold to Rederi AB Torsten, Stockholm, Sweden. (Torsten Carlbom managers) and renamed TORSTEN.
6/10/1954 Sold to Cie del Norte. SA Puerto Limos, Puerto Rica & renamed DORITA.
1958 broken up by Eisen & Metall, Hamburg

CAIRNGOWAN (I) (AS ODDEVOLD) – *World Ship Society*

2. CAIRNDHU (I) (1885-1911)
O.N. 91489   1386 g. 895 n   231 x 34.6 x 17,2 feet
T. 3 Cylinder (18½" x 30" & 48" x 36") engine by Blair & Co. Stockton.120 hp.

5/1885 Launched by H. Edwards & Sons, Newcastle (Yard No.23) for T. Cairns, Newcastle.
1889 Company restyled Cairns & Young. 1891 Company restyled Cairns, Young & Noble.
1903 Company restyled Cairns Noble & Co.
1911 Sold to Otto Banck, Helsingborg, Sweden & renamed ORSA.
15/1/1920 Wrecked at Hallands Vadero, Sweden, on voyage from Malmo to Halmstad in ballast.

3. CAIRNGLEN (I) (1891-1912)
O.N.97964   1565 g 987 n   251 x 36.1 x 16.8 feet
T. 3 cylinder (19", 31" & 51" x 36") engine by Black Hawthorn & Co. Gateshead.158 nhp.

11/3/1891 launched by W Dobson & Co, Newcastle (Yard No.44) for the Cairnglen SS Co., Newcastle. (Cairns Young & Noble, managers).
1903, Managers restyled Cairns Noble & Co.
1912 sold to E Persson, Limhamn, and renamed R. F. BERG.
1915 sold to Olsen & Ugelstad, Norway and renamed DOVREFJELL.
24/2/1917 sunk in collision off Land's End on voyage from Nantes/Ardrossan with a cargo of ore

4. CAIRNAVON (I) (1892-1904)

O.N.97999   1562 g   998 n   250.6 x 36.1 x 16.8 feet.

T. 3 cylinder (19", 31" & 51" x 36") engine by Black Hawthorn, Gateshead. 156 nhp.

26/5/1892 launched by Wood, Skinner & Co, Newcastle (Yard No.37) for Cairn Line of Steamships, (Cairns Young & Noble, managers).

23/1/1901 grounded at the mouth of the Tweed, voyage Huelva to Berwick with a cargo of iron ore. Refloated and repaired (cost £12,000).

1903 Managers restyled Cairns Noble & Co.

14/11/1904 On voyage from Tunis/Antwerp with a cargo of zinc ore, was sunk in collision off Austruweel in the River Scheldt.

CAIRNAVON (I) – *World Ship Society*

5. CAIRNMORE (1892-1913)

O.N.101803   1627 g   1038 n   250.5 x 36.1 x 16.8 feet

T. 3 cylinder. (19", 31" & 51" x 36") engine by Black Hawthorn & Co, Gateshead.156 nhp.

25/7/1892 launched by Wood, Skinner & Co, Newcastle (Yard No.40) for the Cairn Line of Steamships (Cairns Young & Noble, managers).

1903 Managers restyled Cairns Noble & Co.

1913 sold to O.M. Milberg & Co, Christiana, Norway and renamed NORD.

1915 sold to K.S. Nordgren, Bergen, same name.

1917 sold to O.N. Holta, Skien, Norway, same name.

1922 sold to O. Borjesson, Helsingborg, Sweden, same name.

1927 sold to Rederi AB Progress (J.H. Petterson, managers), Helsingborg, Sweden, same name.

1937 sold to J Rang, Tallinn and renamed ARCTURUS, Estonian flag.

14/4/1940 captured by Germans at Bergen and used as supply ship.

22/11/1943 Whilst under tow off Aalesund, attacked by aircraft, damaged and disabled, and was then torpedoed by the Norwegian submarine ULA to the SW of Aalesund with a loss of 8 crew.

CAIRNMORE (AS NORD) – *National Maritime Museum Greenwich*

6. CAIRNROSS (I) (1894-1910)

O.N.104251   1509 g 959 n   255 x 36.7 x 18.1 feet
 T. 3 cylinder. (19", 31" & 51" x 36") engine by G. Clark Ltd. Sunderland. 159 nhp.

21/3/1894 launched by J. Laing & Sons, Sunderland (Yard No. 534) for the Cairn Line of Steamships, Newcastle (Cairns Young & Noble, managers).
12/11/1898 In collision with SS OLDBURG (5006 grt) in River Guadiana, Portugal. Declared a Constructive Total Loss, but was subsequently repaired.
8/1900 On a voyage from Kemi to Christianstad with a cargo of timber, grounded at Skalgrund Kasco. Subsequently refloated and repaired.
1903 Managers restyled Cairns Noble & Co.
5/12/1910 on voyage from Toulon to San Juan, Seville River, went aground at Malabala Point, Tangier, and became a total loss. Sold for £11,000.

7. CAIRNLOCH (1895-1918)

ON.104281   1546 g 959 n   250 x 36.8 x 18.1 feet
T. 3 cylinder. (19",31" & 51" x 36") engine by Black Hawthorn & Co., Gateshead. 158 nhp.

24/4/1895 launched by Short Bros, Sunderland (Yard No. 245) for the Cairn Line of Steamships, Newcastle (Cairns, Young & Noble, managers).
1903 Managers restyled Cairns Noble & Co.
14/3/1906 Ashore at Dakar (£15,000).
1915 Managers restyled Cairns Noble & Co. Ltd.
1918 sold to A. Capel & Co, Newcastle and renamed CAPELBAY, (Cairns Noble & Co. Ltd., managers).
1920 sold to T.B. Stott, Newcastle, same name.
1925 sold to Ignazio Lizzio fu G., Catania, Sicily, and renamed SICILIANO.
1929 sold to Constru. Caroussis and renamed AGH VICTORES.
7/9/1936 Sold for demolition.

8. KEROULA (1895-1903)

O.N.82812   1547 g 1002 n   260.4 x 35.5 x 17.1 feet
C. 2 cylinder (28" x 60" – 39" x 39") engine by G.Clark, Sunderland. 173 nhp.

6/6/1880 launched by S.P. Austin & Son, Sunderland (Yard No. 130) for Porteous & Senior, London, (Avia Steamships Ltd).
1887 transferred to Avis Steamships Ltd., London, (Gilbert Porteous).
1895 sold to Keroula Steamship Co. Ltd., Newcastle, without name change (Cairns, Young & Noble, managers).
19/6/1901 grounded West of Hojens Lighthouse on a voyage from Swansea to Stettin, Baltic, with cargo of coal. Subsequently refloated and repaired.
1903 Managers restyled Cairns Noble & Co.
14/9/1903 wrecked at Segerstad, Oland, Sweden on a voyage from Wyburg to Calais with a cargo of timber.

9. CAIRNLYON (1895-1912)

O.N.81674   1428 g 897 n   249 x 36.1 x 17.5 feet
C. 2 cylinder. (29", & 54" x 36") by J. Redhead & Co., South Shields. 135 nhp

12/8/1882 launched by J. Readhead & Co., South Shields (Yard No. 184) as TRELYON for Edward Hain & Son, St.Ives.
4/9/1895 Sold to Cairnlyon Steamship Company, Newcastle. (Cairns, Young & Noble, managers) and renamed CAIRNLYON.
1901 Transferred to Cairnglen Steamship Company, Newcastle, same managers.
12/8/1901 grounded at Langenberg whilst on voyage from Shields to Stettin, Baltic, with a cargo of coal.
1903 Managers restyled Cairns Noble & Co.
1912 sold to Rederiaktibolaget Anglos, Sweden (A. Johnsson, managers) and renamed ELSIE.
1916 management changed to Carl Norrthon.
1918 Sold to Rederieaktiebolaget M. Modin, Stockholm, Sweden, (H. Modin, managers) same name.
1920 Sold to Johan Bohmann, Gothenburg, Sweden, same name.
1923 Sold to Rederiaktiebolaget Eisie, Sweden (J.Holmstrom, managers), same name.
1935 Sold to Rederiaktiebolaget Fram, Finland, (Algot Johannsen, managers), same name.
12/11/1939 Wrecked off Terschelling whilst on a voyage from Viipuri to Zaandam with a cargo of timber.

CAIRNLYON (AS ELSIE) – *John Clarkson*

10. CAIRNISLA (1896-1915)
O.N.104297   1597 g   1014 n   259 x 36.8 x 18.1 feet
T. 3 cylinder. (19", 31" & 51" x 36") engine by Black Hawthorn & Co., Gateshead. 157 nhp.

16/1/1896 launched by Short Bros, Sunderland (Yard No. 252) for the Cairn Line of Steamships, Newcastle (Cairns, Young & Noble as managers). Completed 3/1896.
1903 Managers restyled Cairns Noble & Co.
24/2/1904 Rescued crew from MARY A TROOP in the North Atlantic.
3/5/1909 Beached near Hook, and subsequently refloated at a cost of £14,000.
1915 Managers restyled Cairns Noble & Co. Ltd.
1915 Sold to Peter Dixon & Company, Grimsby and renamed WEST MARSH but remained under management of Cairns, Noble & Co.
1922 Owners restyled Peter Dixon Steamship Co. Ltd., Oughtibridge, Sheffield, Cairns Noble & Co. Ltd. removed from management.
1930 Sold to N.M. Vericos, Piraeus, Greece and renamed POPI.
1956 sold to Kanso Cia, Naviera, Puerto Limon (Costa Rica) renamed MARY K.
1/12/1957 whilst on voyage from Stratoni to Constantza, sank in the Dardanelles, after the cargo had shifted, all the crew were lost

CAIRNISLA – Painting – *John Band*

11. CAIRNBAHN (1897-1915)

O.N. 81677   1538 g 974 n   259.5 x 36.1 x 17.5 feet

C. 2 cylinder (30" & 58" x 36") engine by J Redhead & Co., South Shields. 161 nhp.

29/10/1883 launched as TREVIDER by J Redhead & Co., South Shields (Yard No. 200) for Edward Hain & Son, St. Ives.

1885 Transferred to the Trevider Steamship Co.Ltd. (Edward Hain & Son, managers)

3/1/1898 Sold to Gaelic Steamship Co., Newcastle (Cairns Young & Noble, managers) and renamed CAIRNBAHN.

5/1900 On voyage from Stettin to Husum, grounded East of Vesterska, Norway. Subsequently refloated and repaired.

1903 Managers restyled Cairns Noble & Co.

23/9/1909 Beached at Faerder, subsequently refloated (cost of repairs £8,000).

1913 Transferred to Cairn Line of Steamships, same name.

1913 Sold to Rederiakitiebolagat Hebe, Helsingborg, Sweden, (C.W. Von Liewen, managers) and renamed IGOR.

1917 Sold to Rederi Akkties Igor (L.Norstrom managers) name unchanged.

1918 Sold to Aktibolagat Svenska America Mexico Line, Gothenburg, Sweden (Dan Bronstrom managers, name unchanged.

17/9/1918 Foundered 10 miles South of the Longstone Light whilst on a voyage from Gothenburg to Hull with a cargo of timber and wood pulp.

12. CAIRNALT (1897-1915)

O.N. 82679   1509 g 969 n   248.8 x 36.1 x 17.5 feet

C. 2 cylinder (29" & 54" x 36") engine by J. Redhead & Son, South Shields. 125 nhp.

5/1892 Launched as SARAH by J. Redhead & Son, South Shields (Yard No. 181) for R. Harrowing of Whitby.

1897 Sold to the Gaelic Steamship Co., Newcastle (Cairns, Young & Noble, managers) and renamed CAIRNALT.

1903 Managers restyled Cairns Noble & Co.

4/10/1905 River Tyne, Northumberland Dock, whilst loaded with a cargo of coal, struck the dock entrance and was beached to prevent sinking. Subsequently refloated and repaired.

1915 Managers restyled Cairns Noble & Co. Ltd.

1915 Sold to V. Damstrom, Borrtelje, Sweden and renamed HERA.

1928 Sold to G.A. Lundberg, Norrtelje, Sweden, name unchanged.

1938 Sold to A. Jansson, Finland, name unchanged.

12/9/1942 Torpedoed by Russian submarine off Mantyluoto, Gulf of Bothnia.

CAIRNALT

13. CAIRNCRAG (1897-1909)

O.N. 101812   3022 g 1951 n   322 x 41.7 x 21.6 feet

T. 3 cylinder (23½", 39", 64" x 42") engine by Hawthorne Leslie & Co., Newcastle. 276 nhp.

20/10/1892 Launched as GREAT NORTHERN by Hawthorne Leslie & Co., Newcastle (Yard No. 314) for The Great Northern Steamship Co. Ltd., Glasgow (J. Coull, Managers).

8/2/1897 Sold to Cairn Line of Steamships, Newcastle (Cairns, Young & Noble, managers) for £22,708 and renamed CAIRNCRAG.

1903 Managers restyled Cairns Noble & Co.

26/7/1909 Wrecked on Dover Island, Cape Canso, Nova Scotia, Canada, whilst on a voyage from Boston to Bathhurst in ballast.

14. CAIRNESK (I) (1898-1899)

O.N. 95465   2073 g 1350 n   279.5 x 37.5 x 19.2 feet

T. 3 cylinder (23", 36" & 60" x 39") engine by Wallsend Slipway & Engineering Co., Newcastle. 226 nhp.

1/9/1889 Launched as KNUTSFORD by C.S. Swan Hunter & Co., Wallsend, Newcastle (Yard No. 133) for the Knutsford Steamship Co. Ltd. (Carlisle & Co., London, managers).

1898 Sold to the Cairn Line of Steamships, Newcastle (Cairns Young & Noble, managers) and renamed CAIRNESK (I).

27/7/1899 Wrecked on Snippan Rocks, Gulf of Bothnia whilst on a voyage from Cronstadt to Pitea (Sweden).

28/8/1899 refloated and whilst under tow, bound for Oskarhamn, foundered off Finngrundet. Total loss.

15. CAIRNMONA (I) (1899-1911)

O.N. 89533   1847 g 1204 n   260 x 36.2 x 20 feet

C. 2 cylinder (33" & 62" x 36") engine by T. Richardson & Co., Hartlepool. 164 nhp.

9/2/1884 Launched as SOUTHWOLD by Short Bros., Sunderland (Yard No. 156) for Southwold Steamship Co Ltd., London (Woods & Lorentz, Managers).

1899 Sold to Cairn Line of Steamships, Newcastle (Cairns, Young & Noble, managers) and renamed CAIRNMONA (I).

1903 Managers restyled Cairns Noble & Co.

3/1911 Sold to A. Hanse-Trove for demolition at Boulogne.

16. CAIRNDON (1900-1915)

O.N. 101993   2692 g 1732 n   299.8 x 40.1 x 20.7 feet

T. 3 cylinder (24", 38" & 64" x 42") engine by T. Richardson & Co., Hartlepool. 266 nhp

6/3/1893 Launched as PHOENIX by Sir Railton Dixon & Co., Middlesborough (Yard No. 382) for Holyhead & Co., London.

1900 Sold to Cairn Line of Steamships, Newcastle (Cairns Young & Noble, managers) and renamed CAIRNDON.

1903 Managers restyled Cairns Noble & Co.

1915 managers restyled Cairns Noble & Co. Ltd.

1915 Sold to The Lowlands Steamship Co., Newcastle (J. Crass & Co., managers) and renamed LOWDALE.

20/4/1917 Captured and sunk by gunfire from U35 in position 90 miles West of Gibraltar whilst on voyage from the Tyne to Tunis with a cargo of coal.

CAIRNDON – *Roy Fenton Collection*

17. CAIRNSTRATH (1901-1917)
O.N. 95455   2128 g 1336 n   280 x 37.5 x 19.3 feet
T. 3 cylinder (23", 35" & 59" x 39") engine by Wallsend Slipway & Engineering Co., Newcastle. 223 nhp

8/1888 launched as FELBRIDGE by C.S. Swan Hunter Ltd., Wallsend, Newcastle (Yard No. 132) for the Felbridge Steamship Co. Ltd., London (W.R. Price & Co., managers).
1901 Sold to Gaelic Steamship Co., Newcastle (Cairns Young & Noble, managers) and renamed CAIRNSTRATH.
1903 Managers restyled Cairns Noble & Co., and again in 1915 Cairns Noble & Co. Ltd.
1917 Sold to Capel & Co. (Newcastle & Hull) Ltd., Newcastle – Cairns Noble & Co. Ltd. retained as managers, name unchanged.
4/8/1917 Torpedoed and sunk by U71 in Bay of Biscay, near St. Nazaire on voyage from Bilbao to the Tyne with a cargo of iron ore. 22 Crew lost, including the Master.

18. CAIRNESK (II) (1902-1911)
O.N. 95802   2237 g 1462 n   285 x 39.2 x 20.2 feet
T. 3 cylinder (21", 33" & 54" x 42") engine by Black Hawthorne & Co., Gateshead. 195 nhp.

25/6/1889 Launched as LECONFIELD by Schlesinger, Davis & Co., Newcastle (Yard No. 153) for G. Sanderson & Co., Hull.
1902 Sold to Cairn Line of Steamships, Newcastle (Cairns Young & Noble, managers) and renamed CAIRNESK (II).
1903 Managers restyled Cairns Noble & Co.
1911 Sold to Otto Banck, Helsingborg, Sweden, and renamed TUVA.
On 6/10/1916 Sunk by German U-Boat off North Cape, Norway.

19. CAIRNTORR (I) (1904-1915) Turret Deck Steamer
O.N. 118628   3588 g 2293 n   340 x 50 x 22.6 feet
T. 3 cylinder (23½", 39" & 66" x 42") engine by Wm. Doxford & Sons, Sunderland. 292 nhp.

19/12/1903 Launched by Wm. Doxford & Sons, Sunderland (Yard No. 314) for the Cairn Line of Steamships, Newcastle, (Cairns Noble & Co., managers).
Completed 1904.
9/1/1907 Whilst at Halifax, Nova Scotia, suffered fire in cargo of cotton. 5,500 bales destroyed (value £150,000).
1915 Managers restyled Cairns Noble & Co. Ltd.
21/3/1915 Torpedoed and sunk by U34 South of Beachy Head whilst on a voyage from Tyne to Genoa, with a cargo of coal.

20. CAIRNAVON (II) (1905-1917)
O.N. 118657   1591 g 1005 n   259 x 36.9 x 18 feet
T. 3 cylinder (19", 30" & 48" x 36") engine by Blair & Co. Ltd., Stockton. 151 nhp.

8/4/1905 Launched by Short Bros. Ltd, Sunderland (Yard No. 325) for the Cairn Line of Steamships, Newcastle (Cairns Noble & Co., managers).
6/1905 Completed.
19/11/1911 Grounded in River Elbe. Subsequently refloated and docked in Hamburg. Repairs £14,000.
8/1914 Requisitioned by Admiralty as Naval supply vessel, name and management unchanged.
1915 Managers restyled Cairns Noble & Co. Ltd.
5/1917 Sold to Christian Salvesen & Co., Leith, name and management unchanged.
3/1919 Released by Admiralty into commercial service and name changed by Salvesen to SOUTRA.
10/1937 Sold to OY Wildfart Ltd, Munksnas, Finland (H. Liljestrand, managers) and renamed EMMI.
1937/1939 Placed under the Estonian flag.
1939/1942 Placed under Finnish flag.
1942 Seized by by German Navy as a prize of war and renamed SCHIRMEK.
4/1942 Used by German Navy as SPERRBRECHER S166.
30/5/1942 Rammed and sunk by s.s OBRA near Kiel Lightship. Subsequently raised and towed to Copenhagen.
15/11/1944 Sunk by saboteurs at Copenhagen.
1945 Raised and broken up.

CAIRNAVON (II) – *Furness Withy Group*

21. CAIRNNEVIS (1905-1917)

O.N. 118660   1587 g 1003 n   259 x 36.8 x 18 feet

T. 3 cylinder (19", 30" & 48" x 36") engine by Blair & Co. Ltd., Stockton 151 nhp.

5/5/1905 Launched by Short Bros. Ltd., Sunderland (Yard No. 326) for the Cairn Line of Steamships (Cairns Noble & Co., managers).

7/1905 Completed.

17/10/1906 Aground at Saltholme, Sweden, subsequently refloated (Repair costs £16,000).

1/10/1909 Damaged in collision with s.s. CYRUS (3368 g/1891). Repaired.

8/1914 Requisitioned by Admiralty as Naval supply vessel, name and management unchanged.

1915 Management restyled Cairns Noble & Co. Ltd.

6/1917 Sold to Christian Salvesen & Co., Leith, name and management unchanged.

3/1919 Released by Admiralty into commercial trade and name changed by Salvesen to TOLSTA.

10/1937 Sold to OY Wildfart Ltd., Munksnas, Finland, (H. Liljestrand, managers) renamed JUSS.

1939 Seized by Spanish Republican Government as a prize of war. Later transferred to Compania Transmediterranea, Cadiz, and renamed CASTILLO GIBRALFARO.

1942 Transferred to Spanish Government ownership, name unchanged.

1948 Sold to Compania de Naviera Vasco Asturiana, Cadiz, name unchanged.

1957 Renamed CARLOS TARTIERE, same owners.

1964 Sold to Societa Metalurgica Duro Felguera SA, Aviles, Spain, name unchanged.

1974 Broken up in Spain.

CAIRNNEVIS (AS CARLOS TARTIERE) – *Hubert Hall Collection*

22. CAIRNRONA (1908-1912)

O.N. 110797   6025 g 3960 n   460 x 52 x 31.2 feet

Post 1908: 7682 g 5012 n   461.5 x 52.1 x 38.7 feet

2 x T. 3 cylinder (22", 37" & 64" x 42") engines by T. Richardson & Sons, Hartlepool. 392 nhp.

3/2/1900 Launched as CONSUELO by C.S. Swan Hunter Ltd., Wallsend (yard No. 251) for Thomas Wilson Sons & Co., Hull. Completed on 5/8/1900.

21/5/1908 Sold to Cairn Line of Steamships, Newcastle (Cairns Noble & Co., managers) and renamed CAIRNRONA (Refitted passenger accommodation, 50 First Class, 800 Third Class). 30/4/1910 Suffered fire at sea off Beachy Head on a voyage from London to Portland, U.S.A. However, 700 passengers transferred to Furness Withy's KANAWA (3886g/1893) which put into Dover and disembarked those persons. Bunkers on fire, later extinguished.

7/5/1910 Arrived London for repairs.

1911 Sold to Cunard Steamship Co Ltd., Liverpool and renamed ALBANIA.

2/5/1911 Departed Southampton for Quebec and Montreal on Cunard's first commercial service to the St. Lawrence River. Did not meet requirements and in 11/1911 was laid up.

1912 Sold to Bank Line of Glasgow (Andrew Weir & Co., managers) and renamed POLERIC.

1929 Sold to Japanese shipbreakers.

6/3/1929 Arrived Osaka, Japan for demolition.

CAIRNRONA (AS CONSUELO) – *National Maritime Museum Greenwich*

23. BELLONA (1908-1912)

O.N. 84134   2932 g 1864 n   340 x 40.2 x 26.8 feet

C. 2 cylinder (41" & 78" x 48") engine by Gourlay Bros., Dundee. 320 nhp.

Post 1887: T. 4 cylinder (19", 41" , 68" x 48") engine by Gourlay Bros., Dundee 353 nhp.

8/7/1881 Launched as WAVERLEY by Gourlay Bros., Dundee (Yard No. 108) for Williamson, Milligan & Co., Liverpool.

1896 Sold to W. Thomson & Co., Dundee and renamed BELLONA.

1908 Sold to the Cairn Line of Steamships, Newcastle (Cairns Noble & Co., managers).

18/11/1908 Aground at Aberdeen on voyage from Montreal to Leith. Refloated and repaired.

31/10/1912 Stranded at Traverse, Newfoundland, refloated next day. 1912 Sold in damaged state to Reid, Donald & Co., Montreal for £9,000.

5/1914 Repaired and renamed DESOLA.

4/3/1915 On voyage from New York to Ardrossan, was destroyed by fire and explosion when cargo of sulphuric acid ignited off Newfoundland.

24. CERVONA (1908-1913)

O.N. 104736   3779 g 2372 n   368 x 45 x 18.8 feet

T. 3 cylinder (27", 43" & 71" x 48") engine by Dunsmuir & Jackson, Glasgow. 396 nhp.

21/9/1896 Launched by Chas, Connell & Co., Glasgow (Yard No. 229) for the S.S. Cervona Co. Ltd., Dundee (W. Thomson & Sons, managers).

1908 Sold to Cairn Line of Steamships, Newcastle (Cairns Noble & Co., managers), name unchanged.

12/12/1913 Wrecked off Fermeuze, Newfoundland on a voyage from Tyne to Portland, Maine, USA.

25. DEVONA (1908-1919)

O.N. 104738   3779 g   2372 n   365 x 45 x 18.8 feet

T. 3 cylinder (27", 43", & 71" x 48") engine by Dunsmuir & Jackson, Glasgow. 396 nhp.

22/10/1896 Launched by Chas. Connell & Co., Glasgow (Yard No. 230) for W. Thomson & Sons, Dundee.

1908 Sold to Cairn Line of Steamships, Newcastle (Cairns Noble & Co., managers).

1915 Managers restyled Cairns Noble & Co. Ltd.

1919 Sold to Williams Steamship Co. Inc., USA and renamed WILLKENO.

1922 Sold to Willkeno-Devona Steamship Co, Callao, Peru.

7/9/1923 Broken up.

DEVONA – *World Ship Society*

26. FREMONA (1908-1917)

O.N. 93470   2922 g   1876 n   328 x 42.2 x 25.9 feet

T. 3 cylinder (26", 41", & 66", x 48") engine by Gourlay Bros., Dundee 295 nhp

15/11/1887 Launched by Gourlay Bros., Dundee (Yard No. 132) for W. Thomson & Sons, Dundee.

1908 Sold to Cairn Line of Steamships, Newcastle (Cairns Noble & Co., managers), name unchanged.

1915 Managers restyled Cairns Noble & Co. Ltd.

31/7/1917 Torpedoed and sunk by U47 off Ushant, France whilst on a voyage from Montreal to Leith with a cargo of grain and timber. 11 Crew lost

27. HURONA (1908-1919)

O.N. 99214   3432 g   2150 n   360 x 44.6 x 26.3 feet

T. 3 cylinder (29", 44", & 71" x 54") engine by Naval Construction & Armament Co., Barrow-in-Furness. 403 nhp.

23/7/1892 Launched by Naval Construction & Armament Co., Barrow-in-Furness (Yard No. 207) for W. Thomson & Co., Dundee.

1908 Sold to Cairn Line of Steamships, Newcastle (Cairns Noble & Co., managers), name unchanged.

1915 Managers restyled Cairns Noble & Co. Ltd.

1919 Sold to Barnett & Co., Cardiff, name unchanged.

24/11/1919 Foundered off Psara, Mediterranean, after being abandoned in heavy weather on voyage from New York to Constanza with a cargo of sugar and general goods.

HURONA – *World Ship Society*

28. IONA (1908-1915)

O.N. 99216   3344 g 2085 n   360.6 x 44.7 x 26.1 feet

T. 3 cylinder (29", 44", & 71" x 54") engine by Gourlay Bros. & Co., Dundee. 408 nhp.

7/9/1892 Launched by Gourlay Bros. & Co., Dundee (Yard No. 155) for W. Thomson & Co., Dundee.

1908 Sold to Cairn Line of Steamships, Newcastle (Cairns Noble & Co., managers).

1915 Managers restyled Cairns Noble & Co. Ltd.

3/6/1915 Captured and torpedoed by U19 off Fair Isle, Scotland on voyage from River Tees to Montreal with general cargo.

29. JACONA (1908-1915)

O.N. 93665   2969 g 1951 n   320.4 x 41 x 19.5 feet

T. 3 cylinder (24", 39", & 64" x 42") engine by J.Dickinson,Sunderland. 285 nhp.

16/7/1889 Launched by J. Laing & Sons, Sunderland (Yard No. 491) as SAINT MARNOCK for the British & Foreign Steamship Co., Liverpool (Rankin & Gilmore, managers).

1899 Sold to W. Thomson & Co., Dundee, and renamed JACONA.

1908 Sold to Cairn Line of Steamships, Newcastle (Cairns Noble & Co., managers)

1915 Managers restyled Cairns Noble & Co. Ltd.

12/8/1915 Mined and sunk off Troup Head, Banffshire, Scotland, with the loss of 29 crew.

30. LATONA (1908)

O.N. 102791   4338 g 2778 n   400 x 47.6 x 26.6 feet

Q. 4 cylinder (25½", 36½" x 52" x 54") engine by Wigham Richardson & Co., Newcastle. 552 nhp.

13/7/1893 Launched as WARRIGAL by Sunderland Shipbuilding Co. (Yard No. 177) for The Blue Anchor Line, London (W. Lund & Co., managers).

1906 Sold to W. Thomson & Co., Dundee and renamed LATONA.

1908 Sold to Cairn Line of Steamships, Newcastle (Cairns Noble & Co., managers).

20/5/1908 Sunk in a collision with the British steamer JAPANIC (3561 g) off the Wolf Rock Lighthouse on voyage from Montreal to London with a cargo of livestock.

LATONA (AS WARRIGAL) – *National Maritime Museum Greenwich*

31. TORTONA (1909-1911)

O.N. 129735   7907 g 4955 n   450.6 x 54.4 x 29.2 feet

2 x T. 3 cylinder (26½", 41" & 68" x 48") engines by Palmers & Co. Ltd., Jarrow. 888 nhp

17/8/1909 Launched by Swan Hunter & Wigham Richardson Ltd., Newcastle (Yard No. 837) for Cairn Line of Steamships, Newcastle (Cairns Noble & Co., managers) for the Cairn Thomson Line service.

3/1911 Sold to Cunard Steamship Co., Liverpool and renamed AUSONIA.

2/1915 Commenced trooping duties Canada/Europe and in 1916 resumed Cunard service.

11/6/1917 Torpedoed by a submarine West of Ireland, but reached port and was repaired.

14/4/1918 Attacked in Atlantic by two torpedoes which failed to hit the ship.

30/5/1918 Disabled by torpedo from U62 in position 620 milesWest of Fastnet. Sunk by gunfire from the U-Boat. Forty four lives lost. Vessel was on voyage from Liverpool to New York. Survivors in lifeboats for 8 days before rescue by HMS ZENNIA.

TORTONA – *National Maritime Museum Greenwich*

32. GERONA (1911)

O.N. 131342   9111 g   5699 n   466.6 x 56.1 x 29.4 feet

2 x T. 3 cylinder (25$\frac{1}{2}$", 41" & 68" x 48") engines by Palmers Shipbuilding & Iron Co., Jarrow. 976 nhp.

6/3/1911 Launched by Swan Hunter & Wigham Richardson Ltd, Wallsend (Yard No. 869) for the Cairn Line of Steamships (Cairns Noble & Co., managers) for the Cairn Thomson service.

3/1911 Contract sold along with the former Thomson Lines, London to Montreal service to the Cunard Steamship Co., Liverpool.

1911 Completed as ASCANIA.

13/6/1918 Wrecked 20 miles East of Cape Ray whilst on voyage from Liverpool to Montreal in ballast.

GERONA (AS ASCANIA) – *National Maritime Museum Greenwich*

33. CAIRNGOWAN (II) (1911-1916)

O.N. 129782   4017 g   2561 n   370 x 51 x 24.6 feet

T. 3 cylinder (24", 40" & 66" x 45") engine by Wm. Doxford & Sons, Sunderland. 292 nhp.

5/10/1911 Launched by Wm. Doxford & Sons, Sunderland (Yard No. 437) for the Cairn Line of Steamships, Newcastle (Cairns Noble & Co., managers).

1911 Completed.

1915 Managers restyled Cairns Noble & Co. Ltd.

20/4/1916 Captured and sunk by gunfire from U69 West of Fastnet on a voyage from Liverpool to Newport News.

34. CAIRNDHU (II) (1911-1917)
O.N. 129786   4019 g 2561 n   370 x 51 x 24.6 feet
T. 3 cylinder (24", 40" & 66" x 45") engine by Wm. Doxford & Sons, Sunderland. 292 nhp.

25/10/1911 Launched by Wm. Doxford & Sons, Sunderland (Yard No. 432) for the Cairn Line of Steamships, Newcastle (Cairns Noble & Co., managers).
1915 Managers restyled Cairns Noble & Co. Ltd.
6/4/1917 Torpedoed and sunk by U40 West of Beachy Head on a voyage from Tyne to Gibraltar with a cargo of coal. Eleven lives lost.

35. CAIRNROSS (II) (1913-1918)
O.N. 133522   4016 g 2513 n   370 x 51 x 24.5 feet
2 x Steam Turbines by Parsons Marine Steam Turbine Co., Newcastle-on-Tyne, geared to a single shaft.

26/11/1913 Launched by Wm. Doxford & Sons, Sunderland (Yard No. 452) for the Cairn Line of Steamships, Newcastle (Cairns Noble & Co., managers)
1913 Completed.
1915 Managers restyled Cairns Noble & Co. Ltd.
28/5/1918 Torpedoed and sunk by U62 NW of Flores, Azores on a voyage from River Tyne to Buenos Aires with a cargo of coal.

CAIRNROSS (II) – *P. N. Thomas Collection*

36. VESPASIAN (1913-1914)
O.N. 92869   2174 g 1374 n   292.6 x 39 x 18.9 feet
T. 3 cylinder (22", 35" & 59" x 42") engine by George Clark, Sunderland. 213 nhp.
Post 1909: 2 x experimental steam turbines manufactured by Parson Marine Turbine Co. Ltd., Newcastle, reduction geared to a single screw shaft.

17/9/1887 Launched as EASTERN PRINCE by Short Bros. Ltd., Sunderland (Yard No. 172) for The Prince Steam Shipping Co., Newcastle.
1895 Owners restyled as Prince Line (1895).
1898 Restyled as Prince Line Ltd.
1907 Sold to Wilson & Watson, name unchanged.
1909 Sold to G. Reid & Co., Newcastle and renamed VESPASIAN.
1909 Sold to Parsons Marine Steam Turbine Co. Ltd., Newcastle, name unchanged. Re-engined as a test bed.
1913 Sold to Cairns Noble & Co., Newcastle.
1914 Hull sold for demolition following the removal of the turbine machinery for fitting into a new hull which had been ordered from Wm. Doxford & Sons, Sunderland. The outbreak of WWI saw cancellation of the project and the new hull, which was partially built, was completed as LORD BYRON for Greek owners.

VESPASIAN (AS EASTERN PRINCE) – *Sea Breezes*

37. CAIRNMONA (II) (1918-1939)

O.N. 140707   4666 g   2806 n   390.2 x 53.1 x 33.7 feet

T. 3 cylinder (28", 46", 75" x 51") engine by Blair & Co. Ltd., Stockton 550 nhp.

29/11/1917 Launched by Sunderland Shipbuilding Co. Ltd., Sunderland (Yard No. 313) for the Cairn Line of Steamships (Cairns Noble & Co. Ltd, managers)

3/1918 Completed.

15/6/1918 Torpedoed off Coquet Island, Blyth whilst on ballast voyage from Leith to Newcastle, 3 crew lost. Towed into River Tyne and subsequently repaired.

23/12/1923 Responsible for rescue of crew of sinking CZARINA in North Atlantic. *Torpedoed by U13 17/10/1939 off Peterhead*

16/11/1935 In River Tyne collided with the Aberdeen trawler DORILEEN.

18/6/1953 Quantity of copper ingots, and the ships propeller, salved from the wreck off Peterhead by salvage vessel TOPMAST 18.

CAIRNMONA (II) – *National Maritime Museum Greenwich*

38. CAIRNVALONA (1918-1952)

O.N. 140718   6402 g   4566 n   415.2 x 53.1 x 25.2 feet

T. 3 cylinder (28", 46" & 75" x 51") engine by Blair & Co., Stockton-on- Tees. 550 nhp.

10/4/1918 Launched by Sunderland Shipbuilding Co. Ltd., Sunderland (Yard No. 314) for the Cairn Line of Steamships Ltd (Cairns Noble & Co., managers) Newcastle.

8/5/1918 Under tow from River Wear to Teesside for engine installation, a torpedo was fired at her, which missed. Vessel was able to continue on into the Tees where the engines were subsequently fitted by Blair & Co. at Stockton.

8/1918 Completed.

24/10/1940 On voyage from Montreal to Tyne, with general cargo, was attacked by aircraft, but escaped serious damage and arrived Leith on 28/10/1940.

9/4/43 Whilst in Convoy ON176, was accidentally in collision with the Norwegian manned destroyer HMS BEVERLEY (Ex USS BRANCH/1920), which sustained severe damage including the loss of her Asdic capability. The warship was unable to keep up with the convoy, and on 11/4/1943 was torpedoed and sunk by U188, with the loss of all but 4 of the ship's company of 152, some of whom were accidentally depth charged by another destroyer escort attending the sinking.

1952 Sold to BISCO for scrap.

30/6/1952 Arrived at Clayton & Davies breaking yard, Dunston-on-Tyne.

CAIRNVALONA – *National Maritime Museum Greenwich*

39. CAIRNDHU (III) (1919-1935)
O.N. 142828   5230 g 3178 n   400 x 52.3 x 28.5 feet
T. 3 cylinder (27", 44", & 73" x 48") engine by Palmer & Co. Ltd., Jarrow. 517 nhp.

1918 Keel laid as WAR CAMEL, a Standard "B" type steamer, by Palmer & Co. Ltd., Jarrow (Yard No. 884)
for The Shipping Controller, London.
1918 Sold to Cairn Line of Steamships Ltd., Newcastle (Cairns Noble & Co. Ltd., managers).
3/1919 Completed as CAIRNDHU (III).
1935 Sold to Livanos Maritime Co. Ltd., Chios, Greece (N.G. Livanos, managers) and renamed STRYMON.
1951 Sold to Compania Maritima International, Liberia, and renamed LIBERTY.
17/1/1952 Wrecked near Pendeen Light, Cornwall, whilst on a voyage, in ballast, from Newport (Mon.) to
La Goulette (Tunisia). Broken up on site.

CAIRNDHU (III) (AS STRYMON) – *National Maritime Museum Greenwich*

40. CAIRNGOWAN (III) (1919-1935)
O.N. 142829   5295 g 3257 n   400 x 52.4 x 28.4 feet
T. 3 cylinder (27", 44", & 73" x 48") engine by Blair & Co., Stockton. 517 nhp.

1918 Keel laid as WAR ORIOLE, a Standard "B" type steamer, by Sunderland Shipbuilding Co. Ltd., (Yard
No. 320) for The Shipping Controller, London.
1918 Sold to the Cairn Line of Steamships Ltd., Newcastle (Cairns Noble & Co. Ltd., managers).
4/1919 Completed as CAIRNGOWAN (III).
9/3/1929 On a voyage from UK to Canada, under Captain Fairley, lost rudder in North Atlantic, approx.
500 miles East of St. John's (Nfld). A jury rudder was rigged and the vessel made St. John's. CAIRNDHU
(III) stood by.
1935 Sold to Bright Navigation Co. Ltd., London, renamed BRIGHT COMET.
1936 Sold to H.C. Wan, Tsingtao, China, and renamed CHI SING.
1938 Sold to Yamashita K.K. of Kobe, Japan, and renamed YAMAHAGI MARU.
12/10/1944 Sunk by US Naval aircraft, SW of Formosa.

CAIRNGOWAN (III) (SS Humber towing Cairngowan, whilst tugs, Mohton and Hugh D assist on port side)
– *Alan Fairley*

41. SCATWELL (1920-1928)

O.N. 132627   4425 g 2763 n   385 x 52 x 25.1 feet

T. 3 cylinder (26", 43", & 71" x 48") engine by J. Dickinson & Sons, Sunderland. 401 nhp.

9/9/1911 Launched a MAISIE by Bartram & Sons, Sunderland (Yard No 220) for Laming D'Ambrumenil & Co., London (A. Laming & Co., managers)

10/1911 Completed.

1917 Sold to Harris & Dixon Ltd., London and renamed SCATWELL.

1919 Sold to Tempus Shipping Co. Ltd.,Cardiff (W.H. Seager & Co., managers), name unchanged.

1919 Sold to Cairn Line of Steamships Ltd., Newcastle (Cairns Noble & Co. Ltd., Managers) name unchanged, as a speculative purchase, for onward sale to Italian interests. Sale terminated by death of proposed buyer, and commenced trading for Cairn Line.

1928 Sold to SA & PA Lemos, Piraeus, Greece and renamed ANTONIOS G. LEMOS.

24/8/1936 Sunk in collision with destroyer HMS KEITH (1400T/1931) South of Portland Bill, on voyage from Danzig to Buenos Aires.

SCATWELL – *Alan Fairley*

42 CAIRNROSS (III) (1921-1940)

O.N. 145449   5494 g 3262 n   425 x 55 x 26.6 feet

3 x Parson Marine Turbines, double reduction geared to a single screw shaft, by Parsons Marine Turbine Co. Ltd., Newcastle

25/11/1920 Launched by The Sunderland Shipbuilding Co. Ltd., Sunderland (Yard No. 322) for the Cairn Line of Steamships Ltd. (Cairns Noble & Co. Ltd., managers).

6/1/1940 Sunk by mine laid by U30 off River Mersey in Convoy OB74 on voyage from Tyne, Leith & Liverpool to St. Johns (NB) with coal & general cargo. Crew all saved.

CAIRNROSS (III) – *National Maritime Museum Greenwich*

43. CAIRNAVON (III) (1922-1925)

O.N. 145487   5248 g 3262 n   400 x 52.3 x 28.5 feet

T. 3 cylinder (27", 44" & 73" x 48") engine by The Central Marine Engine Works, West Hartlepool, 513 nhp.

1918 Keel laid for a Standard "B" Type cargo ship by Wm Gray and Co. (1918), West Hartlepool, (Yard No. 924) for The Shipping Controller, London. Work suspended after war ended.

1919 Sold to Koninklijke Nederlandsche Stroomboot Maatschappij, Amsterdam, (Royal Nederland Steamship Co.) on stocks, and completed 5/1920 as BAARN.

1922 Sold to Cairn Line of Steamships Ltd., Newcastle (Cairns Noble & Co. Ltd., managers) and renamed CAIRNAVON (III).

1/11/1925 Wrecked off Peterhead on voyage from Leith to Montreal with coal and general cargo. 48 Crew and 1 passenger saved.

CAIRNAVON (III) (AS BAARN)

44. CAIRNTORR (II) (1922-1928)

O.N. 145505   5387 g 3206 n   425 x 55 x 26.6 feet

T. 3 cylinder (28", 46½" & 78" x 54") engine by The North Eastern Marine Engineering Co. Ltd., Newcastle. 623 nhp.

10/1922 Launched by Sunderland Shipbuilding Co. Ltd., Sunderland (Yard No. 325) for the Cairn Line of Steamships Ltd Newcastle, (Cairns Noble & Co. Ltd., managers).

11/1922 Completed.

22/10/1928 Wrecked on Island Rock, Coacoacho Bay, Labrador on voyage from Montreal to Newcastle with grain & general cargo.

45. CAIRNESK (III) (1926-1956)

O.N. 149412   5007 g 3015 n   401.8 x 55.3 x 26.3 feet

3 x Parsons steam turbines, double reduction geared to a single screw shaft by The Parsons Marine Turbine Co. Ltd., Newcastle. 530 nhp.

14/4/1926 Launched by Wm. Pickersgill & Sons, Sunderland (Yard No. 216) for the Cairn Line of Steamships Ltd.,Newcastle (Cairns Noble & Co. Ltd., managers).

7/1926 Completed.

30/6/1935 Collided with, and sunk the Dundee registered coaster ERROL (396g/1902) off Inchkeith, Firth of Forth. Coaster was later salvaged.

11/1956 Sold to Vamar Cie. De Nav. Panama, renamed ZERMATT.

1958 Sold for use as an ore carrier and renamed AURORA.

9/1959 Sold for £61,000 and broken up in Japan.

CAIRNESK (III)

46. CAIRNGLEN (II) (1926-1940)

O.N. 149417   5019 g 3024 n   401.8 x 55.3 x 23.3 feet

3 x Parsons steam turbines, double reduction geared to a single screw shaft, by The Parson Marine Turbine Co., Newcastle. 530 nhp.

26/7/1926 Launched by Wm. Pickersgill & Sons, Sunderland (Yard No. 217) for the Cairn Line of Steamships Ltd., Newcastle (Cairns Noble & Co. Ltd., managers).
9/1926 Completed.
23/3/1934 Aground off Caithness. Towed to Tyne and repaired.
22/10/1940 Wrecked off Camel Island, Marsden, 2 miles South of River Tyne. Vessel ran aground on to rocks in fog whilst on voyage from Montreal, Leith to Newcastle with wheat, motor vehicles and foodstuffs. All crew saved. Cargo later salvaged. Total loss.

CAIRNGLEN (II) – *Alan Fairley*

47. CAIRNAVON (IV) (1946-1961)

O.N. 165999   6327 g 4592 n   407 x 54.7 x 33.2 feet

T. 3 cylinder (23½", 37½" & 68" x 48") engine by D. Rowan & Co. Ltd., Glasgow. 439 nhp.

16/12/1940 Launched as EMPIRE SNOW by Chas. Connell & Co. Ltd., Glasgow (Yard No. 431) for The Ministry of Shipping, London (Joseph Costantine Steamship Line Ltd., Middlesborough, managers).
2/1941 Completed.
1/5/1941 Owners restyled Ministry of War Transport.
1943 Cairns Noble & Co. Ltd., Newcastle appointed as managers, name unchanged.
1946 Sold to Cairn Line of Steamships Ltd., Newcastle (Cairns Noble & Co Ltd., managers) and renamed CAIRNAVON (IV).
11/1952 Engines converted from coal to oil burning.
1/5/1956 While berthed at Imperial Dock, Leith, caught fire, 3 crew died.
1961 Sold to Sirikiri Cie. Nav. Panama, Lebanese flag and renamed VERGOLIVADA.
19/9/1966 Stranded on Doganarslan Bank, North Dardanelles with a rope round propeller, on voyage from Novorossiyak, Russia, to Persian Gulf with a cargo of cement. Cargo part jettisoned and trans-shipped.
1/10/1966 refloated and towed to Piraeus, Greece. Laid up.
11/1968 Arrived Shanghai for demolition.

CAIRNAVON (IV) – *National Maritime Museum Greenwich*

48. CAIRNGOWAN (IV) (1952-1969)

O.N. 169233   7503 g 5266 n   428.5 x 60.2 x 34.2 feet

3 x Parsons steam turbines, double reduction geared to a single screw shaft, by The Parsons Marine Steam Turbine Co. Ltd., Newcastle. 4650 shp.

14/12/1951 Launched by Wm. Gray & Co. Ltd., Hartlepool (Yard No. 1248) for the Cairn Line of Steamships Ltd.,Newcastle (Cairns Noble & Co. Ltd., managers).

5/1952 Completed.

1965 Chartered to Manchester Liners and renamed MANCHESTER ENGINEER (III).

1967 Reverted to CAIRNGOWAN (IV) on completion of charter.

1969 Sold to Manato Shipping Co. Ltd., Cyprus. E. Roussos, managers) and renamed GEORGILIS.

10/1973 Arrived Valencia, Spain for demolition.

CAIRNGOWAN (IV) – *William Stanley Wilkinson*

49. CAIRNDHU (IV) (1952-1965)

O.N. 169236   7503 g 5271 n   428.5 x 60.2 x 34.2 feet

3 x Parsons steam turbines, double reduction geared to a single screw shaft, by The Parsons Marine Steam Turbine Co. Ltd., Newcastle. 4650 shp.

9/4/1952 Launched by Wm.Gray & Co. Ltd., Hartlepool (Yard No. 1249) for The Cairn Line Of Steamships Ltd., Newcastle (Cairns Noble & Co. Ltd., managers).

9/1952 Completed.

1965 Sold to Manchester Liners and renamed MANCHESTER EXPORTER (II).

1969 Sold to Halieto Oceanica Naviera SA, Panama (N & J Vlassopulos Ltd., managers) London and renamed GEMINI EXPORTER, Greek flag.

17/5/1971 Broken up at Kaohsiung, Taiwan.

CAIRNDHU (IV) – *Furness Withy Group*

50. CAIRNFORTH (1958-1969)

O.N. 186883   8105 g 4608 n   459.6 x 60.1 x 27.6 feet

4 cylinder SCSA (670mm/2320mm) Doxford Oil engine by Hawthorne Leslie & Co. Ltd., Newcastle.

11/1958 Built by Burntisland Shipbuilding Co. Ltd., Fife (Yard No. 383) for The Cairn Line of Steamships, Newcastle (Cairns Noble & Co. Ltd., managers).

1961 Charter, via Shaw Savill & Albion to the British Phosphate Commission, Makatea.

1965 Chartered to Manchester Liners and renamed MANCHESTER FREIGHTER.

1967 Reverted to CAIRNFORTH on completion of charter.

1969 Transferred to Royal Mail Lines, London, and renamed LOMBARDY.

1970 Laid up in River Fal.

9/1971 Sold to Premier Shipping Co., Singapore and renamed PREMIER PACIFIC.

1975 Sold to Meridian Line SA, Singapore and renamed TARA SEA.

1976 Sold to Sergeant Shipping Co., Greece, and renamed GEORGIOS, Liberian flag.

1979 Sold to Belcore Maritime Corporation, Greece and renamed MASTRO GIORGIS.

15/9/1979 Grounded at Libreville, Gabon, inward bound from Santos. Subsequently refloated and returned to trading.

19/9/1982 Arrived Greece for demolition.

CAIRNFORTH – *National Maritime Museum Greenwich*

5 FURNESS WITHY UNDER SHAW SAVILL & ALBION MANAGEMENT OF CAIRN LINE

SSA 1. CAIRNVENTURE (1969-1974)
O.N. 338899   1436 g   883 n   254.5 x 39.1 x 14.4 feet.
8 cylinder 4 SCSA (320mm x 450mm) oil engine by Atlas-MAK Maschinenbau, GmbH, Kiel, Germany. 1500 bhp.

12.1969 Completed by E.J. Smit & Zoon, Westerbroek, Nederlands (Yard No. 792) for The Cairn Line of Steamships Ltd., Newcastle (Shaw Savill & Albion & Co., London, managers). Chartered to Ellerman Lines.
1974 Sold to Shipmair NV, Rotterdam and renamed SHIPMAIR III.
1976 Sold to Scheepsvaart Maatschappij Passaat Santos, Curacao, and renamed PASSAAT SANTOS.
1977 Sold to Wijdzicht BV, Rotterdam and renamed ERIC.
1979 Sold to Lifestar Cia.Nav SA, Greece (Fereniki Lines, Piraeus, managers) and renamed GHADAMES.
1986 Sold to Brother Hood Shipping Co. Ltd., Cyprus (A. Economides Shipping Ltd., managers) and renamed ALEXIA.
1990 Sold to A.E. Economedes, Cyprus and renamed STAR QUEEN.
1992 Sold to Occidental Cia. Nav. SA., Honduras and renamed VEDIA.
1996 Sold to Occidental Compania Nav. SA, Beirut (Henry Michel Diad, managers), and renamed SHEREEN A.
1997 Sold to A. Economedes Shipping Ltd., Greece, name unchanged. Still in service.

CAIRNVENTURE – *Glasgow University Archives*

SSA 2. CAIRNTRADER (1971-1976)
O.N. 341239   1581 g   977 n   287 x 39.8 x 19.3 feet
8 cylinder 4 SCSA (320mm x 450mm) oil engine by Atlas-MAK Maschinenbau, GmbH, Kiel, Germany. 1600 bhp.

1971 Launched as CAIRNTRADER by E.J. Smit Zoon, Westerbroek, Nederlands (Yard No. 795) for The Cairn Line of Steamships Ltd, London (Shaw Savill & Albion Co. Ltd., managers)
3/1971 Completed as SAXON PRINCE for charter to The Prince Line.
1975 Renamed CAIRNTRADER at end of charter.
1976 Chartered to Prince Line and renamed SAXON PRINCE.
1976 Sold to Van Nievelt, Goudriaan & Co. BV, Rotterdam and renamed ADARA.
1986 Sold to Waterdrive Marine Ltd., Limassol, Cyprus and renamed ANDARA.
1990 Sold to Interfront Shipping Ltd., Cyprus (Rederi AB Hastings, Malmo, Sweden, managers) and renamed PARANA STAR.
1992 Sold to Astarte Shipping Ltd., Cyprus, (Humber Shipping, managers) and renamed PAMELA.
1995 Sold to Shipdepot Ltd., St. Vincent & Grenadines (Rederi AB Hastings, Malmo, Sweden, managers) and renamed ARANA.
1996 Sold to Elreedy Shipping Co., Belize and renamed KARIM I.
2000 Owners now Elreedy Shipping, Egypt, name unchanged.
2003 Same name, same company, Cambodian flag. IMO 7038537. Still in service.

CAIRNTRADER – *Foto Elite Ashford*

SSA 3. CAIRNRANGER (1971-1976)

O.N. 342952   1598 g 1008 n   287 x 39.8 x 17.7 feet

8 cylinder 4SCSA (320mm x 450mm) oil engine Type 8M451AK, by Atlas MAK Maschinenebau, GmbH, Kiel, Germany. 1600 bhp.

11/1971 Completed by E.J. Smit Zoon, Westerbroek, Nederlands (Yard No. 798) for The Cairn Line of Steamships Ltd., London (Shaw Savill & Albion & Co. Ltd., managers).

1976 Sold to Denholm Line Steamers Ltd., Glasgow (J. & J. Denholm, managers) and renamed MOUNTPARK.

1982 Sold to Salverina Varriale, Naples, and renamed BENEDETTO SCOTTO.

1988 Sold to Sadav SP.a., Italy and renamed MARYLAND,

1991 Sold to Commer International, Kingstown, St. Vincent & Grenadines, and renamed SAMER. Still in service.

CAIRNRANGER – *Foto Elite Ashford*

SSA 4. CAIRNROVER (1972-1978)
O.N. 343094   1599 g 1008 n   287 x 39.8 x 17.7 feet
8 cylinder 4SCSA (320mm x 450mm) oil engine Type 8M451AK by Atlas MAK Maschinenebau, GmbH, Kiel, Germany. 1600 bhp.

1972 Launched by N.V. Bodewes Scheepswerft, Martenshoek, Nederlands (Yard No. 512) for the Cairn Line of Steamships Ltd., London (Shaw Savill & Albion Co. Ltd., managers).
1978 Sold to The White Palace Co. SA., Greece and renamed GIANNIS.
1983 Sold to Spartohorion Shipping Co., Greece and renamed ANASTASSIA.
1986 Sold to New Haven Shiping Co. Ltd., Cyprus, and renamed ANASTASSIA ENA.
1986 Sold to Angelamar di Coppola Tommaso, Italy and renamed REIDA.
1993 Sold to Angelamar SAS, Monte di Procida, Italy and renamed STAR.
2000 Sold to Cargo Maritime Inc., St. Vincent & Grenadines and renamed VEGA.
2000 Sold to Trans Oceans Shipping, Panama City, renamed B. VENTURE, Panamanian flag.
2001 Sold to Anquet Marine, Panama City, renamed ALDEBARAN V, Panamanian flag.
2002 Sold to Bolivia, renamed WAGIH I, Bolivian flag.
2003 Sold to Anquet Marine, Panama City, renamed ALDEBARAN V, Panamanian flag. IMO 7127974.
15/9/2003 Still in service.

CAIRNROVER – *Foto Elite Ashford*

SSA 5. CAIRNLEADER (1975-1982)
O.N. 365924   1592 g 1050 n   261 x 44.2 x 18.6 feet
8 cylinder 4SCSA (320mmx450mm) oil engine Type 8M452AK by Atlas MAK Maschinenebau, GmbH, Kiel, Germany. 2400 bhp.

24/6/1975 Launched by Martin Jansen GmbH & Co., K.G. Shiffswerke, Leer, Germany (Yard No. 132) for The Cairn Line of Steamships Ltd., London (Shaw Savill & Albion Co. Ltd., managers).
9/1975 Completed and chartered to Prince Line, same name & managers.
1982 Sold to H. & P. Holwerde, Nederlands and renamed LINDEWAL.
1987 Sold to West Indies Shipping Co. Ltd., Limassol, Cyprus (Holwerde Ship Management B.V., Nederlands, managers), renamed BENED.
1988 Sold to Marinymph Shipping Co. Ltd., Cyprus (Van Nievelt Goudriaan & Co. BV., Rotterdam, managers) and renamed MIRFAK.
1989 Sold to Hecate Shipping Co., Malta and renamed FIVI.
1990-1991 Laid up.
1992 Sold to Great Lakes Marine Co. Ltd., Panama, name unchanged.
2003 Sold to Sea Sun Shipping SA, Comoros, (Sea Lord Maritime, Athens, Greece, managers) and renamed SENTINAL.
19/1/2004 Still in service.

CAIRNLEADER – *Furness Withy Group*

SSA 6. CAIRNFREIGHTER (1975-1982)

O.N. 365994   1592 g   1050 n   261 x 44.2 x 18.6 feet

8 cylinder 4SCSA (320mm x 450mm) oil engine Type 8M452AK by Atlas MAK Maschinenbau GmbH, Kiel, Germany. 2400 bhp.

29/9/1975 Launched by Martin Jansen GmbH & Co., K.G. Schiffswerke, Leer, Germany (Yard No. 133) for The Cairn Line of Steamships Ltd., London (Shaw Savill & Albion Co. Ltd., managers).

1982 Sold to H.P. Holwerde, Holland and renamed TJONGERWAL.

1987 Sold to Rhino Navigation & Co. Ltd, Limassol, Cyprus (Holwerde Ship Management B.V., Nederlands, managers) and renamed CENED.

1988 Sold to Maymorn Shipping Co. Ltd., Cyprus (Van Nievelt, Goudriaan & Co. B.V., Rotterdam, managers) and renamed MEGREZ.

1989 Sold to Albamar S.S. di Luigi & Co., Naples, Italy and renamed VILARO.

1994 Sold to Med Transport S.R.I., Naples, Italy and renamed BLUE LINE.

1996 Sold to Intership Management & Bunker Trading Corp., Madeira, Portugal, and renamed DOMINICA.

1999 Sold to Feldon Business Ltd., Madeira, Portugal and renamed ECUBEA.

2003 Sold to Four Seas Maritime Co. Ltd., Cambodia (Four Seas Maritime, managers) Phnom Penh, and renamed TIKA.

2002 Renamed ABDULRAZZAZ-A

2003 Renamed ABDULRAZZAZ A (no hyphen), same company, managers & Flag. Still in service.

CAIRNFREIGHTER – *Furness Withy Group*

SSA 7. CAIRNCARRIER (1976-1982)

O.N. 366041   1592 g 1050 n   261 x 44.2 x 18.6 feet

8 cylinder 4SCSA (320mm x 450mm) oil engine Type 8M452AK by Atlas MAK Maschinenebau GmbH, Kiel, Germany. 2400 bhp.

2/10/1975 Keel laid.

5/12/75 Launched by Martin Jansen GmbH & Co., K.G. Schiffswerke, Leer, Germany (Yard No. 134) for The Cairn Line of Steamships Ltd., London (Shaw Savill & Albion Co. Ltd., managers)

3/2/1976 Completed.

1982 Sold to Tequila Maritime SA, Panama and renamed TEQUILA SUNSET.

1984 Sold into joint ownership of Shiel & Byrne Ltd. and Arklow Shipping Ltd., Arklow, Ireland (Arklow Shipping Ltd., managers) and renamed ARKLOW BRIDGE.

1988 Sold to Shiel & Byrne Overseas Ltd., Dublin (Arklow Shipping Ltd., managers) name unchanged.

1990 Sold to Boterita Shipping SA, Panama (Navimar SA, managers) and renamed WAVE ROSE.

1990 Navimar SA removed as managers.

1993 Sold to Samer Maritime, Panama (Successors Shipping SA, managers) and renamed ARMOUR.

1997 Sold to Night Flare Navigation SA, Panama (Sigma Maritime Inc., Panama, managers) and renamed EUROLINK.

2001 Managers restyled International Maritime, Greece. IMO 7405091.

2/2004 Now under Mongolian owner, renamed VARUN. Still in service.

CAIRNCARRIER – *Glasgow University Archives*

SSA 8. CAIRNASH (1976-19983)

O.N. 377143   1597 g 1169 n   3200 dwt   275.1 x 46 x 18.4 feet.

Post 1983: 2300 g 1413 n   4028 dwt   301 x 46 x 19.8 feet.

12 cylinder 4SCSA (300mm x 450mm) Fiat oil engine Type GMT by H. Cegielski, Poznan, Poland, geared to a controllable pitched propeller. 2500 bhp.

30/9/1976 Launched by Stocznia Gdanska, Lenina, Poland (Yard No. B473/01) for The Cairn Line of Steamships Ltd., London (Shaw Savill & Albion Co. Ltd., managers).

12/1976 Completed.

1983 Sold to Peter Cremer, Singapore and renamed ANDREA. Vessel lengthened.

1985 Sold to Minibulk Schiffswert GmbH & Co., K.G., Vienna, Austria (Osterreichischer Lloyd/Krohn Shipping Group, managers) and renamed ST. ANTON.

2000 Sold to Bulk Traders International, Phnom Pehn, Cambodia and renamed LEOPARD.

2004 Sold to Hiba Shipping, Syria, renamed NOUR A, Comoros flag. IMO 740564.

21/1/2004 Still in service.

CAIRNASH – *Christopher C. Reynolds*

SSA 9. CAIRNELM (1977-1983)

O.N. 377161   1597 g 1169 g   3200 dwt   275.1 x 46 x 18.4 feet

Post 1983: 2300 g 1413 n   4028 dwt   301 x 46 x 19.8 feet.

12 cylinder 4SCSA (300mm x 450mm) Fiat oil engine Type GMT by H. Cegielski, Poznan, Poland geared to a controllable pitch propeller. 2500 bhp.

19/10/1976 Launched by Stocznia Gdanska, Lenina, Poland (Yard No. B473/02) for The Cairn Line of Steamships Ltd., London (Shaw Savill & Albion Co. Ltd., managers).

1/1977 Completed.

1983 Sold to Peter Cremer, Singapore and renamed CHRISTIANE. Vessel lengthened.

1985 Sold to Minibulk Schiffswert GmbH & Co. K.G., Vienna, Austria (Osterreichischer Lloyd/Krohn Shipping Group, managers) and renamed ST. CHRISTOPH.

20/6/2001 At 0830 hours, whilst Westward bound in the English Channel, the bow of the m.v KONGA collided with the stern of the ST. CHRISTOPH. Both vessels slightly damaged. The 'mind' boggles.

2001 Sold to Bulk Traders International, Phnom Penh, Cambodia and renamed GUEPARD. 2002 Owners restyled Guepard Marine, Phnom Penh, name unchanged, Cambodian flag. Sold to Bulk Traders International, name unchanged, Barbados flag.

2004 Sold to Guepard Marine (Consolidated Bulk), Lebanon, name unchanged, Barbados flag. IMO 7405651.

20/1/2004 Still in service.

CAIRNELM – *Furness Withy Group*

SSA 10. CAIRNOAK (1977-1983)

O.N. 377181   1597 g 1169 n   3200 dwt   275.9 x 46 x 18.4 feet

Post 1883: 2300 g   1413 n 4028 dwt   301 x 46 x 19.8 feet.

12 cylinder 4SCSA (300mm x 450mm) Fiat oil engine Type GMT by H. Cegielski, Poznan, Poland, geared to a controllable pitch propeller. 2500 bhp.

16/11/1976 Launched by Stocznia Gdanska, Lenina, Poland (Yard No. B473/03) for The Cairn Line of Steamships Ltd, London (Shaw Savill & Albion Co Ltd., managers)

2/1977 Completed.

1983 Sold to Peter Cremer, Singapore and renamed LEONY. Vessel lengthened.

1985 Sold to Minibulk Schiffswert GmbH & Co., K.G.,Vienna, Austria (Osterreichischer Lloyd Krohn/ Shipping Group, managers) and renamed ST. JACOB.

2000 Sold to Ronel Shipping Inc., St. Vincent & Grenadines, and renamed JACOB.

2001 Still in service.

CAIRNOAK – *Furness Withy Group*

6 SHIPS ON CHARTER TO THE CAIRN LINE

C1. SCHIAFFINO FRERES/CAIRNAVON (V) (1965)
O.N. 2346 (Liberia)   4414 g 2508 n   410 x 56.1 x 24.1 feet
6 cylinder 2SCSA (720mm x 1250mm) oil engines by Sulzer Bros Ltd.,Winterthur, Switzerland

1951 Launched as TOHORO and completed as APSARA by Van der Giessen & Zonen's Schps., Krimpen, Holland (Yard No. 576) for Cie. Mar. des Chargeurs Reunis, Havre, France.
1958 Sold to Soc. Algerienne de Nav. Charles Schiaffino & Cie., Algiers, and renamed SCHIAFFINO FRERES, French flag.
9/5/1965 – acquired by Furness Withy Group and placed on charter to Cairn Line of Steamships Co Ltd. However on 8.1965 was sold by French company to a Panamanian Company, an associate of Ivanoic and Co Ltd, renamed CAIRNAVON (V), Liberian Flag. Still on charter till 8/1966 Sold to Marbrillo Cia. Nav. SA, Monrovia, Liberia, and renamed ISTINA, Liberian flag.
1969 Sold and renamed JENNY MARINE.
30/10/1969 Damaged by fire, constructive total loss.

SCHIAFFINO FRERES/CAIRNAVON (V) – *World Ship Society*

C 2. MANCHESTER FAITH (I)/CAIRNESK (IV) (1965-1966)
O.N. 300142   4459 g 2456 n   378.2 x 50.4 x 31 feet.
2 x 5 cylinder (480mm x 700mm) 2SCSA Sulzer oil engines Type 5TAG48 by George Clark & North Eastern Marine (Sunderland) Ltd., Sunderland. 7050 bhp (total).

26/11/1958 Launched by Austin & Pickersgill Ltd., Sunderland (Yard No. 435).
3/1959 Completed for Manchester Liners Ltd., Manchester as MANCHESTER FAITH.
1965 Chartered to The Cairn Line of Steamships Ltd., Newcastle (Cairns Noble & Co. Ltd.,managers) and renamed CAIRNESK.
1966 Reverted to MANCHESTER FAITH on completion of charter.
1970 Sold to Marlireas Oceanicas SA, Panama (Aharnai Shipping Inc., New York) (Ilias Konstantinou, Managers)and renamed ILKON TAK, Liberian flag.
1978 Sold to Ilkon Shipping Co. SA, Sarasota,Florida, USA (Same managers) name unchanged.
1978 Sold to Yakinthai Shipping Co. SA, Panama (Chrimar Shipping Co. Ltd., Piraeus, Greece, managers) and renamed CHRYSEIS.
3/6/1983 Broken up at Gadani Beach, Pakistan.

MANCHESTER FAITH (I)/CAIRNESK (IV) – *Furness Withy Group*

C 3. MANCHESTER FAME (I)/CAIRNGLEN (III) (1965-1966)

O.N. 300145   4462 g 2459 n   378.2 x 50.4 x 31 feet

2 x 5 cylinder (480mm x 700mm) 2SCSA Sulzer oil engines Type 5TAG48 by George Clark & North Eastern Marine (Sunderland) Lt., Sunderland. 7050 bhp (total).

22/7/1959 Launched by Austin & Pickersgill Ltd., Sunderland (Yard No. 436)

10/1959 Completed for Manchester Liners Ltd., Manchester as MANCHESTER FAME (I).

1965 Chartered to Cairn Line of Steamships Ltd., Newcastle (Cairns Noble & Co. Ltd., managers) and renamed CAIRNGLEN (III).

1966 Reverted to MANCHESTER FAME (I) on completion of charter.

1970 Sold to Marcaminos Surenos Navegacio SA, Panama (Aharnai Shipping Inc., New York) (Ilias Konstantinou, managers) and renamed ILKON NIKI, Liberian flag.

1978 Sold to Ilkon Shipping Co. SA, Sarasota, Florida, USA, (same managers and name unchanged).

1979 Sold to Tranquil Marine Inc., Panama (Spenco Shipping Co. Ltd., Piraeus, Greece, managers) and renamed EFI.

1980 Sold to Seatime Shipping Inc., Piraeus, Greece and renamed PANAGIS K.

2/1/1981 Damaged in collision with m.v. NORTH WAVE (7848g/1954) whilst laid up at Alexandria, Egypt.

10/1986 Broken up at Alexandria.

MANCHESTER FAME (I)/CAIRNGLEN (III) – *Furness Withy Group*

7 SHIPS TRANSFERRED FROM FURNESS WITHY & CO. LTD TO CAIRN LINE

FW 1. CANOPIC (1969-1973)
O.N. 186452   11,166 g 6350 n   512 x 69.6 x 30.9 feet
2 x 6 cylinder 2SA (750mm x 1500mm) Harland B & W oil engines by Harland & Wolff Ltd., Belfast. 14,300 bhp.

12/1954 Completed by Vickers Armstrong Ltd., Newcastle (Yard No. 151) for Shaw Savill & Albion Co.Ltd., London (Furness Withy & Co. Ltd.).
1967 The Cairn Line of Steamships Ltd. taken over by Furness Withy & Co. Ltd., London.
1969 Transferred to Cairn Line of Steamships Ltd. under new Shaw Savill & Albion management, name unchanged.
1973 Returned to Shaw Savill & Albion Co. Ltd. for disposal.
1975 Sold to Roussos Bros., Cyprus and renamed CAPETAN NICOLAS.
26/12/1981 Laid up at Piraeus, Greece.
27/9/1986 Arrived Alang for breaking up.

CANOPIC – *Foto Elite Ashford*

FW 2. CEDRIC (1969-1973)
O.N. 185253   11,232 g 6,557 n   512 x 69.3 x 30.9 feet.
2 x 6 cylinder (750mm x 150mm) Harland B&W oil engines by Harland & Wolff, Belfast. 14,300 bhp.

11/1952 Completed by Harland & Wolff, Belfast (Yard No. 145) for Shaw Savill & Albion Co. Ltd., London (Furness Withy & Co. Ltd.)
1967 Cairn Line of Steamships Ltd. was taken over by Furness Withy & Co. Ltd., London.
1969 Transferred to Cairn Line of Steamships, Co. Ltd. under Shaw Savill & Albion management, name unchanged.
1973 Returned to Shaw Savill & Albion Co. Ltd. for disposal.
1976 Sold to Fife Shipping Ltd., Panama and renamed SEA CONDOR.
23/1/1977 Aground near Sharjah, UAE, on voyage from Gydnia to Persian Gulf.
25/8/1977 Arrived Koahsiung for breaking up.

CEDRIC – *Foto Elite Ashford*

FW 3. IONIC (1969-1973)

O.N. 300656   11,219 g 6,355 n   512.5 x 70.5 x 30.9 feet.

8 cylinder 2SCSA (750mm x 1500mm) Harland B&W oil engine by Harland & Wolff, Belfast.

3/1959 Completed by Camell Laird & Co. Ltd., Birkenhead (Yard No. 1281) for Shaw Savill & Albion Co. Ltd, London (Furness Withy & Co. Ltd.).

1967 The Cairn Line of Steamships Ltd. was taken over by Furness Withy & Co. Ltd., London.

1969 Transferred to The Cairn Line of Steamships Ltd. under Shaw Savill & Albion Co. Ltd management, name unchanged.

1973 Returned to Shaw Savill & Albion Co. Ltd. for disposal.

1978 Sold to Panorea Shipping Co., Cyprus and renamed GLENPARVA.

1979 Broken up at Kaohsiung.

IONIC

FW 4. LINDFIELD (1977-1980)

O.N. 360757   8,219 g 3,386 n   448 x 66.9 x 22.8 feet.

9 cylinder 2SCSA oil engine by Burmeister & Wain, Copenhagen.

1970 Completed as CAP MELVILLE by Helsing-gor Skibs & Msk., Elsinore, Denmark for the Olau Line A/S, Denmark.

1973 Renamed OLAU ROLF, same company.

1973 Purchased by "K" Steamships Co. Ltd., London (Kaye Son & Co. Ltd., managers), part of Furness Withy & Co. Ltd., London and renamed LIMPSFIELD.

1976 Renamed LINDFIELD, same company.

1977 Transferred to The Cairn Line of Steamships Ltd. (Shaw Savill & Albion Co. Ltd., managers.)

1980 Sold to Cia Argentina de Transportes Maritimos SA, Argentina and renamed MARFRIO.

1995 Sold to Interes Shipping, (Jardine Ship Management Ltd.) and renamed INTERES, Russian flag.

2003 Still in service.

LINDFIELD (AS LIMPSFIELD) – *World Ship Society*

8 SHIPS MANAGED ON BEHALF OF THE BRITISH GOVERNMENT BY CAIRN LINE

MG 1. POLRUAN (1916)
O.N. 136785   3682 g 2370 n   331.0 x 48.3 x 22.0 feet
T. 3 cylinder (24", 40" & 65" x 42.5") engine by The Central Marine Engine Works, West Hartlepool. 292 nhp. Engine No. 744

4/1907 Completed as POLLACSEK by William Gray & Company Ltd., West Hartlepool. (Yard No. 744) for The Atlantic Sea Navigation Company, Fiume, Italy. Austro-Hungarian flag.
1910 Renamed POLNAY. (Same company).
8/1914 Seized by Admiralty at Falmouth.
1915 Taken over by The Shipping Controller, London, and renamed POLRUAN. (Hall Bros/Cairns Noble. Newcastle-upon-Tyne managers). Used as a fleet collier.
25/10/1916 Foundered in North Sea off Whitby, North Yorkshire after colliding with The Whitby Rock, while on a voyage from the Tyne to Dunkirk with a cargo of coal.

POLRUAN (AS POLLACSEK)

MG 2. GEORGIOS ANTIPPA (1917)
O.N. 140671   1960 g 1192 n   265.4 x 35.6 x 20.9 feet
T. 3 cylinder (21½", 36" & 56" x 40") engine by Nederlandsche Stoomb., Maats, Rotterdam, Holland. 250 nhp.

1/1890 Completed as PRINS WILLEM III by Nederlandsche Stoomb., Maats, Rotterdam for Koninklijke West Indische Maildienst, Amsterdam.
1914 Sold to Achaia Steamship Co., Piraeus, Greece and renamed ELPINIKI.
1916 Sold to S.G. Antippa, Greece and renamed GEORGIOS ANTIPPA.
1917 Taken over by The Shipping Controller, London (Cairns Noble & Co. Ltd., Newcastle, managers).
28/11/1917 Torpedoed and sunk in North Sea, off Spurn Head (Humber), by an unknown German U-Boat whilst on voyage from Sunderland to Rouen with a cargo of coal.

MG 3. BORG (1917-1918)
O.N. 94377   2111 g 1662 n   279 x 38.2 x 19 feet.
T. 3 cylinder (21½", 36" & 59" x 39") by N.E. Marine Co. Ltd., Sunderland. 200 bhp.

9/3/1888 Launched as HAMPTON by J.Blumer & Co., Sunderland, for the Commercial Steamship Co., London (Young, Ehiers & Co., managers).
1904 Sold to C.O. Altrichen, Stockholm, Sweden and renamed SVANHILD.
1910 Sold to F.O. Isson, Stockholm, Sweden and renamed ARGUS.
1912 Sold to R. Gohle, Norrkoping, Sweden and renamed BORG.
1917 Taken over by The Shipping Controller, London (Cairns Noble & Co. Ltd., Newcastle, managers), name unchanged.
10/6/1918 Torpedoed and sunk South of Lizard by U103 on a voyage from Bilbao to Jarrow-on-Tyne with a cargo of iron ore. Master & 23 crew lost.

MG 4. WAR POINTER (1918-1919)

O.N. 142341   5267 g   3202 n   400.1 x 52.3 x 28.4 feet.

T. 3 cylinder (27", 44" & 73" x 48") engine by G. Clark Ltd., Sunderland. 517 nhp.

3/1918 Completed by Armstrong Whitworth & Co., Newcastle (Yard No. 932) as a Standard "B" type steamer for The Shipping Controller, London (Cairns Noble & Co. Ltd., Newcastle, managers).

1919 Sold to The African Steamship Co. Ltd., London (Elder Dempster & Co., Liverpool, managers) and renamed BASSA.

29/9/1940 Torpedoed and sunk by U32 in position 500 miles West of County Mayo, Ireland, with the loss of all hands (50 men) in Convoy OB217 on voyage from Liverpool to New York.

WAR POINTER (AS BASSA) – *National Maritime Museum Greenwich*

MG 5. WAR SETTER (1918-1919)

O.N. 142434   5272 g   3195 n   400 x 52.2 x 28.5 feet.

T. 3 cylinder (27", 44" & 73" x 48") engine by G.Clark Ltd., Sunderland. 517 nhp.

6/1918 Completed by Armstrong Whitworth & Co, Newcastle (Yard No. 233) as a Standard "B" type steamer for The Shipping Controller, London (Cairns Noble & Co. Ltd., Newcastle, managers).

1919 Sold to The Cunard Steamship Line, Liverpool and renamed VELLAVIA.

1925 Sold to American-Levant Line, London (S & J Thompson, managers) and renamed RIVER TIGRIS.

5/1931 Sold to Corrado SA di Nav., Genoa, Italy and renamed INES CORRADO.

12/1941 Seized by Argentine Government (Flota Mercante del Estado, Buenos Aires) and renamed RIO DIAMANTE.

1946 Reverted to Corrado SA di Nav., Genoa, Italy and renamed INES CORRADO.

26/7/1951 Scuttled at Porto Vecchio Bay, France when a cargo of coal took fire. Refloated and repaired.

4/1959 Broken up at Tokyo.

MG 6. LIPPE (1919-1921)

O.N. 143148   6714 g 4162 n   452.5 x 59.3 x 28.6 feet.

T. 3 cylinder (32½", 52½" & 86½" x 55") engine by Flensburger Schiffsbau, Flensburg, Germany. 736 nhp.

8/8/1914 Launched by Flensburger Schiffsbau-Gesellschaft, Flensburg (Yard No. 341) for Norddeutscher Lloyd, Bremen,Germany.

2/2/1915 Completed.

2/4/1919 Surrendered to The Allied Control Commission. Allocated to UK and registered at London with The Shipping Controller (Cairns Noble & Co. Ltd., Newcastle, managers)

1/2/1921 Sold to the Hain Steamship Co., St. Ives and renamed TRESITHNEY (E.Hain & Son, managers)

16/11/1922 Collided with steamer CARLMO KJELLBERG (644g/1883) when leaving Antwerp for Australia.

17/11/1924 Sold to The Federal Steam Navigation Co., London (New Zealand Shipping Co., managers) and renamed PIPIRIKI.

15/11/1929 Grounded at Swansea on arriving from Port Pirie. Later refloated.

12/1929 to 7/1930 & 2/1931 to 11/1933 Laid up in River Fal.

9/11/1933 Sold for £7,300 to Ditta L. Pittaluga Vapori, Genoa, Italy, for demolition. Arrived Genoa 3/12/1933 and broken up in 1934.

MG 7. TILLY RUSS (1919-1920)

O.N. 143342   2775 g   1764 n   291.4 x 41.3 x 18.6 feet.

T. 3 cylinder (20$\frac{1}{2}$", 35$\frac{5}{8}$" & 55" x 35") engine by A.G. "Neptun" Rostok, Germany. 229 nhp.

18/2/1905 Launched by A.G. "Neptun" Rostok, (Yard No. 238) for E.Russ, Hamburg.

3/1905 Completed.

1919 Surrendered to UK – The Shipping Controller, London (Cairns Noble & Co. Ltd., Newcastle, managers).

25/10/1920 Purchased by The Ellerman Wilson Line, Hull and renamed MANCHURIAN (Ellerman Lines, Liverpool, managers).

6/5/1925 Sold to Ellerman Lines Ltd., London, (Ellerman Lines, Liverpool, managers), name unchanged.

8/1934 Sold to Wards, Sheffield for demolition.

7/12/1934 Arrived Milford Haven for breaking up.

MG 8. TOTMES (1919-1921)

O.N. 143353   4618 g   2775 n   473 x 61.2 x 28.7 feet.

T. 3 cylinder (29$\frac{1}{2}$", 48$\frac{3}{8}$" & 80$\frac{5}{8}$" x 55") engine by A.G. Neptun, Rostock, Germany. 484 nhp.

7/1914 Completed by DDG Kosmos, Hamburg (Yard No. 338)

4/8/1914 Interned at Antwerp. 1/11/1918 Taken over by The Shipping Controller, London.

2/5/1919 Cairns Noble & Co. Ltd., appointed as managers.

1921 Sold to The David Steamship Co., London and renamed St. ALBANS ABBEY.

1921 Sold to the United Netherlands Steamship Co., Rotterdam and renamed ARENDSKERK.

3/1935 Sold to Soc. Per Azoni Cantiere Navale Breda, Venice and renamed ERNESTO.

1943 Seized by Germany (Mittlemeer Reederi GmbH, managers), same name.

1945 Returned to previous Italian owners.

1952 Sold to Enrico Insom Fu Antonio, Rome, Italy, same name.

6/5/1954 Grounded at Muroran, Japan on voyage from Hampton Roads, USA, to Japan.

24/6/1954 Refloated and broken up at Osaka.

TOTMES (AS ERNESTO) – *National Maritime Museum Greenwich*

MG 9. EMPIRE BRIGADE (1940)

O.N. 135157   5154 g   3189 n   400 x 53.5 x 26.6 feet

T. 3 cylinder (27", 44$\frac{1}{2}$" & 74" x 48") engine by Blair & Co, Ltd., Stockton. 440 nhp.

11/1912 Completed by Priestman & Co., Sunderland (Yard No. 239) as HANNINGTON COURT for The Court Line, London (Haldinstein & Co., managers).

1936 Sold to Achille Lauro, Naples and renamed ELIOS.

10/6/1940 taken as war prize at Newcastle and handed over to Ministry of War Transport, London (Cairns Noble & Co. Ltd., Newcastle, managers), renamed EMPIRE BRIGADE.

18/10/1940 Torpedoed and sunk by U99 in Convoy SC7 (Sydney, Nova Scotia/UK) West of Hebrides on voyage from Montreal to Tyne. 8 Crew and 1 gunner lost.

MG 10. EMPIRE SAILOR (1940-1942)

O.N. 168024   7061 g   4460 n   430.8 x 55.4 x 27.6 feet

Post 1937: 6086 g   3806 n

6 cylinder 4S.SA oil engine by Stabilimento Tecnico, Trieste. 2500 bhp.

Post 1937: 6 cylinder 4S.SA Fiat oil engine by Lloyds Austriaco, Trieste. 5800 bhp.

5/1926 Completed as CELLINA by Stabilimento Tecnico, Trieste for Navigazione Libera Triestina S.A. (The Libera Line).

1/1/1937 Ownership transferred to Italia Societa Anonima di Navigazione, Genoa (Italia Line). Altered and re-engined.

10/6/1940 Arrested at Gibraltar after war contraband inspection. Brought to UK by Ministry of War Transport and placed under the management of Cairns Noble & Co. Ltd., Newcastle. Renamed EMPIRE SAILOR.

21/10/1942 Torpedoed and sunk by U518 in West bound Convoy ON145, from Liverpool to New York. During the voyage several ships left the convoy for various other ports, the EMPIRE SAILOR left the convoy to sail to St John NB, when approximately 300 miles east of Halifax was torpedoed (see page 37). Captain Fairley, (who was in command of the CAIRNMONA (II) when she was torpedoed in 1939) was among the survivors.

EMPIRE SAILOR (AS CELLINA) – *National Maritime Museum Greenwich*

MG 11. BLACK OSPREY (1940-1941)

O.N. 216012   5852 g   4436 n   409.6 x 54.1 x 27.1 feet

GEC Steam turbines, double reduction geared to a single screw shaft by The General Electric Corporation, Schenectady, New York, USA. 508 nhp.

2/1918 Completed as the WEST ARROW by the Skinner & Eddy Corporation, Seattle, USA (Yard No. 12) for The United States Shipping Board (Emergency Fleet Corporation) for The Black Diamond Lines Inc., New York.

1935 Sold to the Black Diamond Lines Inc., New York and renamed BLACK OSPREY.

5/9/1939 Detained for 8 days in UK port (NE Atlantic Sector) on war contraband inspection, and then released, nothing found.

13/11/1939 Again detained for 8 days in UK port (NE Atlantic Sector) on war contraband inspection, and released, nothing found.

1940 Sold to Ministry of Shipping, London (Cairns Noble & Co. Ltd., Newcastle, managers)

18/2/1941 In Convoy HX107 East bound from Halifax N.S. to Newport (Mon), became a straggler with engine trouble and was torpedoed and sunk by U96 South of Iceland with a cargo of steel, and vehicles. 25 Crew lost.

BLACK OSPREY – *World Ship Society*

MG 12. BLACK CONDOR/EMPIRE LAPWING (1940-1942)

O.N. 168093   5358 g 3386 n   400.7 x 54.2 x 30.4 feet

2 x Steam turbines, double reduction geared to a single shaft by The Westinghouse Electric & Manufacturing Co., Essington, Pennsylvania, USA. 661 nhp.

1/1921 Completed as ALA by The Merchant Shipbuilding Corporation, Harriman, Pennsylvania (Yard No. 39) for The United States Shipping Board (Emergency Fleet Corporation).

1931 Sold to American Diamond Lines Inc., New York, name unchanged.

1935 Sold to The Black Diamond Lines Inc., New York and renamed BLACK CONDOR.

17/9/1939 Detained for 8 days in a UK port (NE Atlantic Sector) on war contraband inspection, nothing found, released.

5/11/1939 Again detained for 8 days in UK port (NE Atlantic Sector) on war contraband inspection. Released after cargo and mail had been removed.

1940 Sold to The Ministry of Shipping, London (Cairns Noble & Co. Ltd., Newcastle, managers).

1941 Transferred to Ministry of War Transport, London, (same managers), renamed EMPIRE LAPWING. [After Ministry of Shipping and Ministry of Transport merged on 1/5/1941, they restyled as The Ministry of War Transport]

1942 Transferred to the Belgian Government in exile in London (Cie. Maritime Belge [Lloyd Royal] S.A., London, managers) and renamed BELGIAN FIGHTER.

9/10/1942 Torpedoed and sunk by U68 off Cape Town, South Africa with a loss of 5 crew.

MG 13. EMPIRE SNOW/CAIRNAVON (IV) (1943-1946)

For full details of this vessel, please refer to Cairn Line Fleet List, No. 47.

EMPIRE SNOW – *National Maritime Museum Greenwich*

9 SHIPS MANAGED ON BEHALF OF OTHER COMPANIES BY CAIRN LINE

M 1. WEST MARSH/CAIRNISLA (1915-1922)
For Peter Dixon & Co., Grimsby.
Full details of this vessel, please refer to Cairn Line Fleet List, No. 10.

M 2. SOUTRA/CAIRNAVON (II) (1917-1919)
For Christian Salvesen & Co. Ltd., Leith.
Full details of this vessel, please refer to Cairn Line Fleet List, No. 20.

SOUTRA – *Graeme Somner*

M 3. TOLSTA/CAIRNNEVIS (1917-1919)
For Christian Salvesen & Co. Ltd., Leith.
Full details of this vessel, please refer to Cairn Line Fleet List, No.21.

M 4. CAIRNSTRATH (1917)
For Capel & Co. (Newcastle & Hull) Ltd., Newcastle
Full details of this vessel, please refer to Cairn Line Fleet List, No.17.

M 5. CAPELBAY/CAIRNLOCH (1918-1920)
For A. Capel & Co. (Newcastle & Hull) Ltd., Newcastle
Full details of this vessel, please refer to Cairn Line Fleet List, No. 7.

The rest is history.

10 AWARDS GIVEN TO MERCHANT NAVY PERSONNEL SERVING DURING THE SECOND WORLD WAR IN THE CAIRN LINE

M.V. EMPIRE SAILOR
Built 1926, 6,086 GRT, British, Cargo Tramp, Ministry of War Transport

London Gazette on 8th June 1943 for services when the ship was torpedoed and sunk.

HENDERSON, Alexander	Chief Officer	M.B.E. (Civil)
JONES, William Charles	Mess Room Steward	Commendation
STAMPS, Frank	Second Officer	Commendation

S.S. CAIRNESK (III)
Built 1926, 5,007 GRT, British, Cargo Tramp, survived the war

London Gazette on 4th June 1943 for Birthday Honours 1943

| ORGAN, Ellis Arthur | Master Mariner | O.B.E. (Civilian) |

Captain Organ's son Ellis was 2nd Mate on the BLACK OSPREY which was torpedoed on 18th February 1941. He was one of the 24 crew lost.

Note: During research, came across an Ellis Michael Organ, born 18th June 1936 who served as a Cadet/3rd mate on board the CAIRNDHU (IV) from 10th December 1952 to 7th December 1956. He is the son of Ellis Organ and the grandson of Captain Ellis Arthur Organ.

| GUILD, Andrew | Boatswain | B.E.M. (Civil) |

S.S. CAIRNVALONA
Built 1918, 4,929 GRT, British, Cargo Tramp, Survived the war.

London Gazette on 4th January 1944 for New Year Honours 1944

| GROVER, Thomas | Donkeyman | B.E.M. (Civil) |

London Gazette on 15th June 1945 for Birthday Honours 1945

| BERTRAM, Thomas Alexander | Chief Engineer | O.B.E. (Civil) |

11 EPILOGUE

Over the years, I have seen vast changes in Dock and Harbour facilities, through lack of shipping, being greatly depleted in ports like Newcaste Upon Tyne, Leith, Grangemouth, Middleborough, Liverpool, Hull, Manchester, Southampton and London, plus others compared to the trade in the 1950's and 1960's. However freight container terminals were created eg. Teesport, Felixstowe, Southampton and London. To date these above named freight container terminals are starting to lag behind to similar facilities available on the continent. If not expanded or new sites created in the UK, the imports/exports of this country may have to be shipped to larger Docks in the Continent instead of the UK. At present there are planning applications for new freight container schemes in the 'pipeline' – one site in Southampton has recently been refused due to environmental problems. Promoters of other sites are more optimistic, sites are planned for the 'London Gateway' near Thurrock, Essex. Another at Felixstowe South (UK largest Container Dock) and in Harwich, Bathside Bay. Permission will have to be granted as soon as possible (promised by March '05) so the schemes can get started. If not the UK will lose out again.

Our Merchant Navy from 1950's to-date has been decimated to a large degree, there are not many British ships left, if any, I bet it's a foreign country owns it or controls it e.g. QUEEN ELIZABETH 2, Cunard Line, – controlled from Miami, U.S.A., owned by the Carnival Corporation. I realise that we do have certain shipping companies still operating from the U.K. but it's the number of companies and tonnage that have dramatically dropped although I observe that ships are larger and mainly freight container type. I believe that on some instances, under a few of the countries that are classed with 'flag of convenience' safety regulations and rules are lax and I suspect a few ships sail without being properly sea-worthy, or otherwise as from time to time we hear of ships sinking.

In June 2001, a report came out from the Marine Accidents Investigations Branch, that safety recommendations are being overlooked on purpose by some Shipping Companies, in order to reduce costs. In doing so, lives of personnel are in danger from death or injuries. Standards have dropped to a level, where 1453 accidents were reported to the M.A.I.B. during the year 2000, and deaths went from 25 to 45 in U.K. waters and on British ships abroad. Accidents rose from 107 in 1999 to 140 in 2000, up to 2004 there is no improvement.

In the annual report of M.A.I.B., Rear Admiral John Lang, the Chief Inspector of Marine Accidents, reported that several accidents are due to commercial pressures and therefore a contributory factor. He also stated that poor safety standards are the root cause, as some shipping companies go too far in order to make a profit. The shippers go after the cheapest options, and there is availability of sub-standard ships, owned by people who are also un-concerned about cutting operating costs. There are also companies who reduce training, basic maintenance, and cut back on staff on ships to dangerous levels.Adml. Lang also reported on the fishing industry which had a very bad year in 2000, whereupon 39 U.K. registered vessels and 32 fishermen lost. Primarily through pressures on the fishing vessels, regarding cuts in quotas and terrible weather, making fishermen to push their luck too far in cutting corners. I read in a National newspaper, where, anyone, without qualifications or required sea time experience, can purchase a ship's Deck Officer's Certificate. For £3,000, plus your name, and age, you can receive a Certificate through a 'third party' who has contact with a 'department' in an 'unknown country'. How much of a check is made, I don't know, but the holder of such a 'Certificate', can apply for a job and if accepted, be in charge (on watch etc.,) of a small or large cargo ship, tanker or a passenger ship – 'Lord forbid'. I believe the British Mercantile Authorities are very strict, but one could slip through the 'net', I assume these 'bogus' people go abroad for jobs. Before anyone accuses me of scare mongering, just think, it happens in all walks of life. There are people who have a certain knowledge of what is required, but either can't/won't study or pass examinations, and they take the 'short cut'. The problem is of course, there are always people who will oblige and supply the necessary documents (for cash of course). Thankfully they are usually found out, till some time has passed, but it is hard to believe that this actually happens.

In the United Kingdom, one reason for the shortage of properly qualified officers, are less young people are coming forward to take up a career in our Merchant Navy. The shrinking of our country's shipping tonnage doesn't help, even although the ships appear to be built larger but less of them. I know of a Merchant Navy Officer with his Master's Certificate (sailed as 1st Mate) who left the M.N. and joined a Police Force (change of career) in the 1980's. Six years later, he thought better of it, so he resigned and applied to be re-instated into the M.N. Thinking, because of his six years away, he might be lucky and get a job on a smallish cargo ship or tanker. He was surprised to say the least, when offered and accepted a First Officer's navigation position on a large passenger liner. We are at times, apart from our present shipping companies, in a state of relying on other countries shipping, in bringing quite a lot of cargoes to and from the United Kingdom. Cruise ships are certainly coming into their own, taking back what the Airlines did to them, back in the 1960's, 70's and up to date, cruising is a leisurely form of travel, than flying out to spend a period of time in one place.

I shouldn't forget British Shipbuilding, once the best in the world. I am not sure what position the U.K. is in the World ranking of ship builders, but someone did mention to me, it was about 30th. (I ask you?)

To think of the very fine ships this country has built, from passenger, cargo, tankers, ferries and even tugs. Recently I read that from 2001 to 2004, world wide, that 54 cruise ships will be built. ' NOT ONE IN THE UNITED KINGDOM'. More is the pity; we were unable to obtain the construction of the QUEEN MARY 2. In November 2002, the keel of the QUEEN MARY 2 was laid in the yard of Chantiers de L'atlantique at St.Nazaire, France for delivery in 2003. It is now in service. There were plans for Italy to build another Cunard ship – THE QUEEN VICTORIA, in a Venice Shipyard, for service in 2005, but this new building has been transferred to a sister company, P & O Cruises, and will be named ARCADIA. A new 85,000 ton vessel will be built, also in Italy, to be named QUEEN VICTORIA, and will enter service in 2007. Both aforementioned are under the control of the U.S. owned Carnival Corporation.

So what has gone wrong with this country, do we blame the shipping companies, shipyards, our past or present Governments. I do believe that progress must move forward, that the best yards must build the required ships, at reasonable and competitive pricing for cargo or passenger ships or any type of ship but where does that leave the UK?

'WHERE AND WHY HAVE ALL THE BRITISH SHIPS GONE?'

Note: INTO THE FUTURE

For several years now, different countries have been involved in building larger ships. So far there have been 1st, 2nd and 3rd Generation Container ships, (in turn the ships are built bigger.) The Maersk Container Shipping Company at present is operating 3rd Generation Container ships, which are capable of carrying approximately 7,600 containers.

There is the concept of intellectual reasoning of forward planning, for building 4th Generation Container ships that will carry cargoes of 10,000 containers, or more. These ships will circumnavigate the world, stopping off at only certain ports, some experts believe that there might be about 6 ports in the world that will accommodate these 'massive' ships.

In turn, the cargoes will then be shipped to other ports, on possibly 2nd and 3rd Generation Containers ships that can enter and unload their cargo, therefore the 2nd/3rd Generation Container ships could be used as 'feeder' ships to the 4th Generation Container ships. There is a problem that the 'lifting cranes' at present ports, would not be able to reach over the width of the ship to lift a container. In Singapore, they now have a crane that can 'reach' over the width of 22 containers, they are certainly 'looking into the future.' The Panama Canal Authority is already in the process of planning the building of new locks of vastly increased dimensions to cope with future phases of larger vessels. The mind 'boggles' at the thought of what size these ships will become in the years to come.

MARBRILLO CO.NAVIERA_PANAMA
M/V"CAIRNAVON" -LIBERIAN
PORT OF REGISTRY:MONROVIA
OFFICIAL NO: 2346

CREW LIST

No.	Name and Surname		Rank	Age	Nationality	Pass.No.
1.	Vinko	Racic	Master	64	Yugoslav	692067
2.	Ivica	Morsti	Ch.Off.	35	Yugoslav	473308
3.	Grgur	Depolo	2nd.Off.	37	Yugoslav	968751
4.	Mato	Stanovic	3rd.Off.	28	Yugoslav	886983
5.	Peter	Wallace	Supercargo	30	English	103195
6.	Patrick	Doyle	R. O.	18	English	
7.	Mario	Viduoic	Bosun	44	Stateless	35141
8.	Nikola	Majkovica	A. B.	24	Yugoslav	1043796
9.	Videslav	Jarolimev	A. B.	30	Stateless	37673
10.	Lizcardo	Aviles	A. B.	31	Spanish	780248
11.	Jose	Maneiro	A. B.	33	Spanish	36590
12.	Branko	Milat	A. B.	27	Yugoslav	1042249
13.	Dinko	Bobio	A. B.	29	Yugoslav	1087851
14.	Sreoko	Grgin	O. S.	27	Yugoslav	1087859
15.	Nenad	Brzic	O. S.	29	Yugoslav	1087808
16.	Vazmoslav	Sersic	Ch.Eng.	57	Yugoslav	863215
17.	Marin	Sivio	1st.Asst.	27	Yugoslav	1037454
18.	Ive	Videka	2nd.Asst.	26	Yugoslav	1088519
19.	Josip	Fabris	3rd.Asst.	35	Yugoslav	1078870
20.	Marijan	Gabrijan	Greaser	58	Stateless	29217
21.	Ivan	Lovrin	Greaser	30	Yugoslav	473281
22.	Emilie	Garcia	Greaser	24	Spanish	956263
23.	Milan	Bojanic	Wiper	23	Yugoslav	1047374
24.	Drageslav	Mario	Wiper	24	Yugoslav	835351
25.	Krste	Orljenko	Ch.Cook	36	Yugoslav	560990
26.	Ante	Barcul	2nd.Cook	25	Yugoslav	820281
27.	Milan	Galic	Messboy	22	Yugoslav	1007872
28.	Milan	Stojanic	Ch.Stew	26	Yugoslav	423472
29.	Slavko	Smoljan	Messboy	21	Yugoslav	1087806
30.	Ivan	Baric	Messboy	21	Yugoslav	442183

M A S T E R

Capt.Vinko Racic

13 Appendix 2

CAIRN THOMSON LINE

CANADIAN SERVICE
THE CAIRN LINE OF STEAMSHIPS LTD

SCHEDULE OF SAILINGS SUMMER SEASON JULY TO DECEMBER 1965

VESSEL	LEITH	NEWCASTLE	MIDDLESBROUGH	GRANGEMOUTH	QUEBEC MONTREAL	TORONTO HAMILTON	MONTREAL QUEBEC
CAIRNESK	JULY 5–7	JULY 8–11	JULY 12–14	JULY 15–16	JULY 25–29	JULY 31–AUG. 3	AUG. 5–10
CAIRNGLEN	JULY 20–22	JULY 23–26	JULY 27–29	JULY 30–31	AUG. 9–13	AUG. 15–18	AUG. 20–25
CAIRNAVON	AUG. 4–6	AUG. 7–10	AUG. 11–13	AUG. 14–15	AUG. 24–28	AUG. 30–SEPT. 2	SEPT. 4–9
CAIRNESK	AUG. 19–21	AUG. 22–25	AUG. 26–28	AUG. 29–30	SEPT. 8–12	SEPT. 14–17	SEPT. 19–24
CAIRNGLEN	SEPT. 3–5	SEPT. 6–9	SEPT. 10–12	SEPT. 13–14	SEPT. 23–27	SEPT. 29–OCT. 2	OCT. 4–9
CAIRNAVON	SEPT. 18–20	SEPT. 21–24	SEPT. 25–27	SEPT. 28–29	OCT. 8–12	OCT. 14–17	OCT. 19–24
CAIRNESK	OCT. 3–5	OCT. 6–9	OCT. 10–12	OCT. 13–14	OCT. 23 27	OCT. 29–NOV. 1	NOV. 3–8
CAIRNGLEN	OCT. 18–20	OCT. 21–24	OCT. 25–27	OCT. 28–29	NOV. 7–11	NOV. 13–16	NOV. 18–23
CAIRNAVON	NOV. 2–4	NOV. 5–8	NOV. 9–11	NOV. 12–13	NOV. – 22		DEC. – 1
CAIRNESK	NOV. 17–19	NOV. 20–23	NOV. 24–26	NOV. 27	DEC. – 6		DEC. – 14
CAIRNGLEN	DEC. 2–4	DEC. – 5					
CAIRNAVON	DEC. 10–12	DEC. – 13					
CAIRNESK	DEC. 23–26	DEC. – 27					

Thereafter on Winter Service to St. John N.B./Halifax N.S.
A Schedule will be issued in October.

Cargo can be accepted in Transit Shed at any time prior to Shipment by arrangement with Port Agent

UNITED KINGDOM
Newcastle
Middlesbrough — Cairns Noble & Co. Ltd.
Leith
Grangemouth — Furness Withy & Co. Ltd.
Glasgow
Dundee — R. M. Beveridge & Co. Ltd.

CAIRNS NOBLE & CO. LTD.,
Milburn House,
Newcastle upon Tyne, I.

CANADA
Montreal
Toronto
Halifax — Furness Withy & Co. Ltd.
St. John N.B.
Hamilton
Quebec — Ramsay, Greig & Co. Ltd.

Telephone: Newcastle 24225
Telex: 53414 Corgowise N/Tyne
Telegrams: Gowan

For Freight, Bookings, Rates etc., apply Agents

MANAGERS

ABSTRACT OF FINANCIAL FEATURES: THE CAIRN LINE OF STEAMSHIPS LTD NEWCASTLE-UPON-TYNE
FOR THE YEARS 1955 - 1965

YEAR	NOMINAL CAPITAL	ISSUED CAPITAL	PREFERED SHARES	ORDINARY OR DEFFERED SHARES	DEBENTURE STOCK	CAPITAL RESERVE
	£	£		£		£
1955	1,500,000	600,000	-	600,000	-	300,000
1956	1,500,000	600,000	-	600,000	-	507,316
1957	1,500,000	600,000	-	600,000	-	557,316
1958	1,500,000	600,000	-	600,000	-	357,316
1959	1,500,000	600,000	-	600,000	-	300,000
1960	1,500,000	600,000	-	600,000	-	275,000
1961	1,500,000	600,000	-	600,000	-	300,000
1962	1,500,000	600,000	-	600,000	-	300,000
1963	1,500,000	600,000	-	600,000	-	300,000
1964	1,500,000	600,000	-	600,000	-	300,000
1965	1,500,000	600,000	-	600,000	-	238,258

YEAR	PROFIT ON TRADING AND INVESTMENTS	FOR YEAR ENDING	DIVIDEND ON ORDINARY SHARES ON PARENT CO.	DIVIDEND ON ORDINARY SHARES OF PREVIOUS YEAR	BOOK VALUE OF FLEET AND PROPERTIES	RESERVE & BALANCE CARRIED FORWARD
	£				£	£
1955	174,756	31/12/1955	10%	7.50%	965	374,463
1956	174,756	31/12/1956	12.50%	10.50%	1,089	386,827
1957	162,425	31/12/1957	12.50%	12.50%	1.427.118	376,720
1958	41,026	31/12/1958	5%	12.50%	1.479.965	362,067
1959	47,795	31/12/1959	5%	5%	1.404.891	238,339
1960	92,694	31/12/1960	5%	5%	1.330.858	232,658
1961	48,197	31/12/1961	2.50%	5%	1.256.203	227,155
1962	21,465	31/12/1962	2.50%	2.50%	1.218.143	210,274
1963	61,753 (LOSS)	31/12/1963	2.50%	2.50%	1.144.686	139,333
1964	39,537 (LOSS)	31/12/1964	2.50%	2.50%	1.070.494	90,983
1965	16,654 (LOSS)	31/12/1965	2.50%	2.50%	824	65,519

15 SHIP INDEX

16 GENERAL INDEX

Notes